Florida Ramble

Florida Ramble

Alex Shoumatoff

Vintage Books
A Division of Random House, Inc.
New York

To Leslie, Willie, and Baby Natasha

FIRST VINTAGE BOOKS EDITION, JANUARY 1990

Copyright © 1974 by Alex Shoumatoff

Library of Congress Cataloging-in-Publication Data
Shoumatoff, Alex.
Florida ramble / Alex Shoumatoff. — 1st Vintage Books ed.
p. cm.
ISBN 0-679-72579-2
1. Florida—Description and travel—1951–1980.
2. Shoumatoff, Alex—Journeys—Florida.   I. Title.
[F316.2.S5 1990]
917.5904′6—dc20 89-40094
CIP

Manufactured in the United States of America
10 9 8 7 6 5 4 3 2 1

Contents

Acknowledgments

Many people who do not actually appear in this book have helped in the writing of it. I would particularly like to thank Dr. and Mrs. Archie Carr and their sons, Tom and Steve, for inspiring me with their love and concern for the wild beauty of native Florida; Winfred Grandy, the eminent deltiologist, who generously allowed me to chose from his collection of postcards, estimated conservatively at one million, many of those that appear in this book; and Nach Waxman, my editor, without whose good-natured guidance at every stage of its creation, this book would never have seen the light of day.

Goodbye north
Hello south
Goodbye north
Hello south
It's so cold up here
the words freeze in your mouth

I'm goin' to Florida
where I can have my fun
I'm goin' to Florida
where I can have my fun
where I can lay out in the green grass
and look up at the sun

"Florida Bound Blues"

Panama
City

Apalachicola

Bristol
(Garden
of Eden)

☆ Tallahassee

St. Augustine

Devil's
Millhopper

Payne's
Prairie

The Bight

Crystal R.

Oklawaha R.

St. Johns R.

red-cockaded
woodpecker
nest

Art-
Grindles
Statue
Eva.

Silver
Springs Shores

Ashram

Disney
World

Cape
Kennedy

Hillsborough

Giant's
Camp

Frostproof

Zolfo
Springs

Peace R.

Canal C-38

Lake
Okeechobee

Hobe
Sound

Caloosahatchee R.

Immokalee

Sanibel
Island

Corkscrew Swamp

Tamiami Trail

Ecological Disaster Area

Miami
Beach

Tiger
Camp

Everglades

Florida
Bay

Key Largo

N

W   E

S

Map by N. A. Shoumatoff

The Land Where Climate Is King

One day I was rummaging around in my father's wastebasket when I came across a big bright-orange envelope. Inside was an invitation to a dinner for a new "fully planned" development in Florida called Silver Spring Shores. There was a number to call if you were interested.

So I phoned in my RSVP and, a few weeks later, drove over to nearby Mt. Kisco, New York, reporting, as directed, to a small private room above David's Restaurant-Bar, where the dinner was being held. As I walked in, a big lady done out in white leather hotpants, white go-go boots, and a tight blouse came up to me with an ingratiating smile. "Hi," she said, "I'm Julie." Julie and I sat down at a table covered with a red-and-white-checked plastic cloth, and she explained that she was going to be my "personal consultant" for the evening. At another table, a white-haired lady sat with a little man in a shiny gray suit, who, I guessed, was *her* consultant. There were a few more tables, but the prospects for whom they had apparently been set up never showed, so we had the place to ourselves. Without any further delay, a waitress brought in a three-course meal consisting of Swiss steak, cole slaw, and a cube of orange Jello with a squirt of whipped cream. The four of us sat there, eating and making stabs at conversation.

Dinner behind us, we sat back and watched a movie called *Something New Under the Sun*. As it began, the narrator, a man I recognized from a well-known denture cream commercial, was standing in front of some whirring spools, which, he explained, were "hungry computers." These machines, he said blinking solemnly, had figured out that the United States needs a hundred and ten new cities to keep up with the population projected for the year 2000. Then the scene shifted to Silver Springs Shores, where a group of "peaches," as bathing belles are known in Florida, was revealed gracing the edges of a pool. Then there was an artistic shot of the sunlight being filtered through the fronds of some palms, and the narrator's voice came in again. "And Silver Springs Shores is one of these new cities," he said.

The movie lasted about ten minutes, and when it was over, Julie got up and slipped around to my side of the table. With a well-practiced movement, she opened up her black business bag and took out a contract. Then she started to talk very fast, so fast I could hardly make out what she was saying, but I got the feeling I was being exposed to what is known as high-pressure salesmanship.

"When you put your money in the bank, what do they do?" she began. "They buy land, of course. So why don't you buy land yourself? If you hang onto it till your kids go to college, that in itself will pay for them. Twenty years ago Miami Beach was going for peanuts. Today you couldn't buy the length of this table for twenty grand."

Over at the next table I could hear the little man in the shiny gray suit stepping up his pitch to the white-haired prospect. At one point I heard him purr to her, "They say Florida adds ten years to your life."

Meanwhile Julie painted me a few more tempting word pictures, but they fell on deaf ears. What could I say? I just wasn't about to "deposit." I could tell she was getting pretty disgusted.

The white-haired lady, though, was beginning to weaken. After a few more minutes with her consultant, she finally succumbed and wrote out a check which ensured, to avoid any possible confusion, that a sign bearing her own name would immediately be planted on a third-of-an-acre lot at Silver Springs Shores. I told Julie it sounded mighty intriguing, but I guessed I'd have to go down to Silver Springs Shores and look the place over for myself.

So a few weeks later I threw my belongings into the trunk of my Oldsmobile convertible, bade farewell to my friends and loved ones, and did just that.

On the way down, cruising the interstates, I read billboards to pass the time. Somewhere in Georgia I started to notice ones celebrating Silver Springs Shores, a "Distinctive, Total Community" down in "The Land Where Climate Is King." By the time I got to Marion County, Florida, there were Silver Springs Shores signs at every junction, offering free orange juice to all comers. They led across the broad swells of the Central Highlands, over miles of dry, sandy pasture and palmetto scrub, past a succession of thoroughbred-horse farms, and finally up to a Polynesian-style building with a sign in front that said, SILVER SPRINGS SHORES WELCOME STATION. I went in. A cute young thing in a pleated orange skirt was waiting at the door with a tray on which there were Dixie cups full of orange juice. I took one and downed it gratefully. She put down her tray and took me to the office of Bill Plum, the community's "housing consultant."

Bill sat at a desk behind pictures of his wife and teen-aged daughter and told me to make myself at home. He'd just been transferred here from Arizona, where the AMREP Corporation, the large conglomerate that is behind Silver Springs Shores, is putting up a new city called Rio Rancho Estates. "I've been selling model homes on and off for the last twenty years," he said with a congenial grin. On the wall was a map of the eighteen-thousand-acre property which the AMREP Corporation had recently bought from Arthur Godfrey. Bill pointed out the central plant where sewage received tertiary treatment, the greenbelt of live oaks which separated ten nonpolluting companies in the industrial park from the residential area, and some of the other features that made Silver Springs Shores "ecology-protected." He proudly described how the original trees had all been spared, and how the roofs of some of the houses had even been notched to provide room for them to grow. Then he looked me dead in the eye and said, "We figure you can get twenty-five thousand homes in here without destroying the natural character of the place."

Bill and I went out to the parking lot, got into his Buick estate wagon, and headed for the model home village. On the way we drove along an eighteen-hole golf course which, Bill explained, had been designed by the leading English golfing architect, Desmond Muirhead, to weave in and out of the development. As we passed

three women in curlers tearing down the first fairway in a golf cart, Bill took the opportunity to invite me to a bingo game that night at the Silver Springs Shores Yacht Club. The club was located on a big lake in the back of the property. The Silver Springs Shores people, Bill told me, had poisoned out the native gizzard shad in the lake and restocked it with Florida big-mouth bass, and they were in the process of dredging out twenty more bodies of water. "Well, I'll be," I thought to myself, "I guess that must be why they call it Silver Springs Shores."

The homes in the model village were simple cinderblock ranchhouses, which had taken from ninety to a hundred and twenty days to build. The tropical plantings around them had been grown in the development's own nursery with the help of human waste recovered by the sewage-treatment plant—another ecological plus. You could choose your house from a number of models with names like the Malta ("for real luxury living this house has it all!"); the Mariposa ("charming columns lend an open, breezy look!"); the Hibiscus ("lots of room to play—a lot of house for the money!"), the Primavera, the Largo, the Osprey, the Palmetto, the Cameo, the Suwannee, the Ponce de Leon, the Boxwood, the Cypress, the De Soto, the Mimosa, and the Byerly. Any original ideas for the "house of your dreams" had to be approved by the Silver Springs Shores Corporation.

We went into one that was called the Pinecrest, a cozy little number with two bedrooms, a two-car garage, a pantry, and an optional sauna bath. When we came out again, I noticed a little clump of white mushrooms that had sprouted on the lawn. Being something of a mushroom buff, I stooped down and ascertained from their satin white innocence, from the frills on the upper part of their stems, and from the bags on their bottoms that they were none other than *Amanita virosa,* the so-called Destroying Angel, a lethal fungus, which, when ingested, first produces hilarity, then convulsions, and finally knocks you dead within twenty-four hours. "Holy crow," Bill gasped when I told him this. "We'd better get them out of here," I suggested. So we wrapped them up in a Kleenex and put them in the disposable litter bag in his Buick.

Bill had to get back for a rendezvous with some prospects, so I told him I could take care of myself and thanked him for the tour. He drove back to the Welcome Station, and I went to see if I could hunt up some of the people who had already moved in. So far only two hundred and fifty homes had been built, and they had been bunched up along a system of curvilinear, cul-de-sac-type streets. Behind them, as far as I could see, roads sectioned off the rolling hills, and mounds of sand had been dumped where other houses would soon stand. There were six hundred pioneer residents in this small community, which was expected in time to balloon into a megalopolis of sixty-five thousand. Most of the people hailed from subdivisions and cities in the North. Forty percent were retired. They'd only been there for a year and a half, but their neighborhood had already taken on a completed, lived-in look. They had mowers, inflated plastic pools, and jungle gyms in their yards; tools, paint cans, and appliances in their garages. Their lawns were green and healthy; many were being sprinkled at that very moment.

The first door I knocked on was opened by a man who squinted at me for just a moment, then said, "Sorry, bub, we don't want any," closing it in my face without another word.

In the next block I met a retired tool and die maker from Chicago standing in his driveway. "I'm satisfied, but my wife ain't," he told me. "We been here a year and a half. The people think they're big shots but they don't have a pot to pee in. This is dog eat dog. We haven't talked to our neighbors since the first day we moved in. We put up a fence for our dog so they put up a higher one. They said they were gonna sell their house to a nigger. I said niggers are better than some white folks anyway." On his neighbor's front lawn there were three plaster flamingoes.

Pretty soon the man's wife, a little white-haired lady in shorts, came out to see what was up. Far from being as he had described, she seemed delighted with Silver Springs Shores. "You can wear anything you want. People wear bikinis. Course I can't swim, but I have a lot of friends. Well-to-do friends, too." Down the block the lawn in front of one house was brown and shriveled. It had obviously not been watered in some time. I asked the lady about this. "Oh, the folks who lived there moved back to San Antonio last month. They didn't like it here. But she was one of them chronic complainers."

On the next block a boy was peddling around the house in a toy tractor. "Your dad in?" They were going to church in a few minutes, but his dad let me in and I sat at a breakfast bar drinking a glass of water and watching a pack of cars streak down a speedway on the television while they got ready. "We like it here," said the man of the house, who had been working for an electronics company since he had gotten out of the Marines. The company had recently transferred him to their new plant, one of the ten nonpolluting companies in the industrial park. He said he had grown up on a farm in Minnesota, one of ten kids. He didn't play golf and barely knew how to swim. "When I was a boy we didn't have planned activities like they got here at the community center." His wife, who looked a bit haggard but was still quite a beauty, also spoke highly of the community center, but complained that she had to drive six miles to Ocala to shop.

As the family drove off for evening mass in their Galaxie, I got back in my convertible and took in the rest of the development. At the far end of it I came to a place where the rolling terrain finally leveled out into a vast plain. There were no houses on it yet, but the plain had already been divided into streets, and the streets had already been paved and named. I parked on the edge of it, under a lone shade tree, and watched the day end in a distant cloudbank. The nighthawks, or bullbats, as they are called around here, had come out in the failing light, and were banking and swooping all around me, making eerie whirs with their wings. A dozen shimmering white and silver egrets filed across the sky toward their roost in some big oak or pine. Several kinds of frogs and crickets started up in the grass, and were joined by the monotonous z of cicadas in the shade tree. Fresh salt breezes coming off the Gulf of Mexico more than fifty miles to the west rolled in as it grew dark. A carload of teenage dates parked nearby and made out while their tape deck poured psychedelic music into the darkness. I got out and roamed the various lanes, courts, ways, and terraces, reading their names. A full moon slipped up through the trees. I went back to the car, stretched out in back, and dropped off.

The land that is turning into Silver Springs Shores was once part of an open "piny woods," which covered the coastal plains of the South until the arrival of European man—one solid stretch of widely spaced longleaf pines, a hundred and twenty feet high. The floor of this forest was carpeted with wire grass and numerous vines, flowers, and shrubs, which were regularly swept out by fire. To the settlers accustomed to the dark, dense forests of the North, the piny woods must have seemed more like an endless park or clearing through which they could ride for days at a time, bathed in sunlight. The choice land to settle was the windblown sandhills of longleaf pine, rather than the dry, tangled understories of the pine flatwoods or the big scrub. On these gently rolling, well-drained slopes, a man could raise a few crops, because the sand was underlain with an impermeable layer of clay called citronelle, which had washed down from the Appalachians several million years earlier. Longleaf was prime timber in this part of the world: a fire-, disease-, and insect-resistant wood with incomparable tensile strength and adhesive qualities. First, the Spanish and the English harvested it for "naval stores," and the era of transoceanic commerce began with ships whose masts and spars were longleaf and whose cracks were plugged with its gum. Then the turpentine industry came into the woods, bleeding the trees from Vs cut upon the trunk as high as a darkey could reach. Special field hollers and shouts were composed by the gangs of blacks as they collected the turpentine in pots and poured it out into barrels. Salty old rednecks then drove the barrels out of the woods, conducting teams of mules or oxen with rawhide whips, for which they came to be known as "crackers." An accomplished cracker could use his whip to brush a fly from an ox's ear, silence a rattlesnake at five paces, or send a hound dog yelping through the massive colonnades of pine. But then the pulp and paper industry moved into the piny woods and wiped out the largest stands of longleaf, replacing them with inferior but faster-growing slash and loblolly pine. Other industries took their toll. The tree, according to Harrar and Harrar's *Guide to Southern Trees,* was, and still is, in hot demand for the manufacture of "paints, varnishes, furniture and shoe polishes, japans, soaps, cloth-printing inks, pharmaceutical preparations, greases, specialty lubricants, sealing wax, roofing materials, brewer's pitch, and sweeping compounds." By the 1920s longleaf, the prince of southern pines, no longer dominated the hilly uplands of central Florida and could only be found on a few "islands" in the scrub, as Marjorie Kinnan Rawlings called them in her books about this region. Today there are no piny woods to speak of. What have not been cleared for cattle or citrus trees have been subdivided and cemented over beyond recognition.

So if you now wanted to get some perspective on Silver Springs Shores, you'd have to go into the Ocala National Forest and hunt for a few sandhills with longleaf still on them. But the forest has 366,291 acres, and you could probably spend the rest of your life looking for a longleaf pine without finding anything but sand pine. The Ocala forest is the largest contiguous stand of sand pine in the world.

Not having quite that much time, I got hold of the Forest Service, and they arranged for me to go out one morning with one of their men, Ben Sanders. Ben is in his early thirties, smokes a Missouri Meerschaum corncob pipe and speaks in a lackadaisical drawl which seems to let on to only part of what he is thinking. Beside him, on the seat of his green pickup, he keeps a crumpled straw hat for whenever he comes across a squatter in the forest and has to look official. We headed down a sandy road that followed an ecotone, or type line between two different plant communities.

On our right was the hot, dry sand-pine scrub of the Ocala Forest. The sand pine, which normally shades the lower growth, had been harvested, leaving the turkey oaks, along with a few other scrawny oaks—myrtle oaks, Chapman oaks, and sand live oaks—to bake in the full sun. We stopped and Ben showed me how the turkey oaks had adapted to the direct sunlight by turning their leaves perpendicular to the ground so they wouldn't be scorched.

On the left was what we were looking for: a longleaf island, one of the five in the northern part of the forest. Every once in a while, as we drove the three-mile length of the island, we would pass a little dome of live oaks that had managed to escape fire long enough to form a closed canopy and change the microclimate beneath them to one that discouraged longleaf and favored themselves. Growing under the longleafs there were turkey oaks, heavily bearded with Spanish moss, some of which had got to be thirty feet tall because there hadn't been any fire on the island in years. There were other signs that fire had been absent and that the scrub was moving in: dog fennel, persimmon, deer moss, and other "invaders." We got out of the pickup and started walking through the open, sunny woods. The ground was littered with huge longleaf cones, or "burrs," as Ben called them. I picked up a broken turpentine pot. "Bet that's fifty years old," Ben said.

We sat down beside a longleaf that was about sixty feet high, with a clean, straight trunk whose bark was split into orange-brown plates. In the crown, shiny needles, eight to eighteen inches long, hung in clusters of three. Maybe twenty and twenty-two feet up two holes had been bored into the tree. The bark around the bottom of one was coated with a glazed patch of gum. "If we wait here you jes' might get to see a red-cockaded woodpecker," Ben said in a low voice.

The floor of the woods where we sat was mostly covered with wire grass, but it was also host to a large variety of other herbaceous plants: partridge pea, white snakeroot, Alicia's pea, Florida beggarweed, Queen Anne's delight, and wild indigo, just to name the ones in the immediate reach of Ben's arm. Since he moved down from the mountains of North Georgia five years ago, Ben has quietly assimilated the Latin names of most of the plants that grow in the forest. "Here's an interesting one," he said, snatching up a sprig of *Ceanothus microphyllus*. "Florida's version of New Jersey tea." We inspected a lichen with gray-green stalks and bright red tips called British soldiers. Overhead, a fox squirrel with a bunch of leaves in his mouth was frozen upside down on a branch, flicking his bushy brown tail. "They're getting scarce," Ben said, stirring the needles on the floor with the stem of his corncob. Just below the surface was clean white sand. It was amazing that anything was growing here, let alone a full-scale forest. One factor in the area's fertility is clay several feet down. The other, Ben explained, is directly under the wire grass, in a maze of fungus filaments called mycorrhizae which spread silently along the forest floor in search of decaying animal and vegetable matter. These intricately woven strands trap decomposing organic litter before it is leached out into the sand, breaking it down into simple minerals, then transferring it directly to the roots of the plants. Without the mycorrhizae it is clear there would be no forest. Further, there might well also be no Ocala deer herd. The mushrooms, which are the fruiting bodies of the fungus form about ten percent of their diet. Several yards away a small, partially nibbled purple mushroom had cropped up in the wire grass. I ventured a guess that it was a *Hypholoma perplexum,* the so-called perplexing hypholoma. Ben said he didn't know but he'd take my word for it.

The longleaf islands are called "fire subclimax communities" because wild fire keeps the oaks from taking them over and turning them into hammocks, or stands of hardwoods. Periodically, fire

sweeps the forest floor, cleaning out the oaks, but leaving the tall longleafs, which have thick, flame-resistant bark and reserves of starch stored in a deep taproot to maintain themselves against conflagration. The fire also spares the "grass stage" of the longleaf, a shock of needles that stands only a foot high for its first six to ten years; but it destroys the spores of the brown spot needle blight, a fungus that attacks them.

The animals that live on the longleaf islands are mainly ones that can flee, fly, or burrow away from fire. The Florida gopher turtle and the gopher frog, for example, have adopted a burrowing way of life because it is the only way they can survive in the community. The pocket gopher probably moved in from the Southwest, along with the diamondback rattlesnake and the prickly-pear cactus, as the dunes of the Central Highlands were formed. It is an important member of the community, because in the process of tunneling it leaves mounds of leached-out nutrients on the surface where the plants can use them again. Certain other animals have not been as helpful, such as the Florida razorback hog, which was introduced by the rural Spanish and loves to root the longleaf. But the rural crackers of Georgia and Florida have pretty much taken care of the hog problem by staking out the countryside into "hog claims." Each stakeholder is entitled to gun down any feral pig that sets foot in his claim. Turkeys are also occasional visitors, and the majestic, illusive sandhill crane, as his name suggests, sometimes browses in the piny woods.

Ben and I were still waiting to see the pair of red-cockaded woodpeckers. The longleaf we were watching was their tree. They returned to it every year and made a new hole, puncturing the bark around it to the skin to make the gum run. Why they did this was a mystery, but they would never lay their eggs till the gum was oozing freely around the hole, even though it made the nest more conspicuous and their belly feathers were denuded by incubating the sticky eggs.

These birds are very fixed in their ways. They nest only in living longleaf pines that have contracted red heart rot, which can strike the tree after anywhere from fifty to five hundred years. Nobody knows how they can tell which trees have the disease, but they may do it simply by tapping the trees and detecting the sound of the rot in it. In any case, these woodpeckers once ranged widely through the South, but when the piny woods began to disappear, so did they. Up until recently, the foresters, who were conscientious about keeping a "clean forest," would walk through the longleafs and cut down every tree with an oozing hole in it, because they knew it had red heart rot. After tremendous agitation by a few conservationists, the foresters were persuaded that the diseased trees were doing no harm and should be left standing for the red-cockaded woodpeckers. The birds were declared rare and endangered by the Audubon Society, and now whenever a forester comes across a tree of nesting red-cockaded woodpeckers, he marks it with a band of red paint and it is left alone. The International Paper Company has set aside sanctuaries for the bird, and there are now sixty protected nests near Georgetown, not far from where we were.

The higher of the two holes in the woodpecker tree had apparently been abandoned by the red-cockaded 'peckers because they couldn't get the gum to flow around it any more. But we could hear the incessant frail screaming of young inside. By and by a woodpecker with a beetle in its beak sailed up to a branch in front of the hole, its dazzling red head, white belly and wing patches, and glossy blue-black back standing out in the sunlit browns and greens and yellows of the forest. But it wasn't a red-cockaded woodpecker, which is actually one of the least striking woodpeckers, with only a thin gash of red across the back of its neck. It was a red-*headed* woodpecker. These birds too were almost wiped out about thirty years ago, when a bounty was placed on them because they destroyed telephone poles. But since the practice of creosoting poles the red-headed woodpeckers have come back strong. You often see them in clearings, because they aren't afraid of people.

The red-*cockaded* 'pecker, on the other hand, is "a might skittish," as Ben put it, and adept at the woodpecker trick of slipping around to the other side of the tree when he sees you coming. The best time to see one is early in the morning, and your best bet is to set up some kind of a blind. "Still," Ben said, "when they've got young to feed, they'll come to the tree no matter who's there." We listened but all we could hear was the little red-headed nestlings screaming in the upper hole. The red-cockaded young must have gone off to practice flying. We kept listening for their call note, which one bird book describes as being "in a decidedly fretful tone—as if the bird were constantly in an irritable state of mind." But everything seemed pretty contented here on the island, and hearing nothing to match that description, we finally pulled out. We had better things to do than wait for a bird who wasn't going to show.

The Lay of the Land

What exactly Florida is doing there, so queerly appended to the North American continent, is still under investigation. The latest theory is that it was just left there by Africa a hundred and eighty million years ago, when a giant land mass made up of North and South America, Europe, and Africa started to come apart and make way for the Atlantic Ocean. The proponents of this "continental drift" theory contend that certain Paleozoic sandstones thousands of feet below the Central Highlands of Florida are dead ringers for ones that lie in Paleozoic basins east of the Mauritanide Mountains of northwest Africa. They report finding trilobites—small, extinct sea creatures, among the first forms of life to have eyes—fossilized in these sandstones. Some of these creatures, they maintain, are members of the same genus, and there is little likelihood that such similar trilobites could have arisen as far away from each other as they are now. And then there's the fact known to every schoolchild, that the continental margins of west Africa and eastern North and

South America have an amazing resemblance to each other, like adjacent pieces in a jigsaw puzzle. An additional fact is that when they are matched up Florida fits snugly against what is now Guinea and Sierra Leone. Finally, the continental-drift people argue, the very structure of North America suggests that Florida is not an original part of it: they point to the way, for example, the Appalachian Mountain chain sweeps southwest into Alabama and Mississippi and eventually peters out in the Ouachita Mountains of Arkansas and Oklahoma completely avoiding Florida; and the way certain magnetic changes occur at the top of the peninsula, indicating that Florida is entirely a separate structural province.

However it got there, the peninsula seems to have taken on its present shape at least a hundred and thirty-five million years ago. The whole thing is a plateau maybe four hundred miles long and three hundred wide, part of which—the state of Florida—is now above water, and the rest of which is a broad shelf, as big again as the state, lying off in the Gulf of Mexico and teeming with marine life.

As the Atlantic Ocean opened, the theory goes, the original Florida plateau of quartzitic sandstones and crystalline granites gradually subsided, and the Gulf Stream poured over it like a wide, shallow river. Then, about sixty-five million years ago, layers of limestone began to accumulate on the sunken plateau. The process was a common one. Calcium carbonate precipitated out of the seawater and was extracted from it by shellfish and coral polyps which needed it to build the hard parts of their bodies. Certain lime-secreting algae helped, too, in pinning down floating particles of calcium carbonate and starting accumulations. The skeletons of polyps stacked up in time and became reefs. The shells were ground into a fine calcareous ooze called marl or crushed into a frozen mash called coquina. Other contributors of their bodies to the land-building process were huge marine mammals, now extinct, who left their teeth and bones in beds scattered around the state. These concentrations now account for about eighty percent of the nation's phosphate.

For most of its history the Florida plateau was cut off from North America by a swift northerly current which flowed in the vicinity of Jacksonville through a channel called the Suwannee Straits. Finally, twenty-five million years ago, a convulsion took place that uplifted the middle of the plateau into the Central Highlands and diverted the Florida current southward to its present channel below the Keys, where it makes as much as six knots today. From then on, Florida was no longer an island. Streams encroached from the mainland, washing down ill-sorted sands, yellow and yellow-red stream gravels, organic swamp deposits, green and blue-green clays, and other eroded matter from the Appalacians.

In the last five million years five glaciers have crept down on the continent. Although they never got as far south as Florida, they had dramatic repercussions there. As the glaciers advanced, a great deal of the sea's water was caught up in ice, and the broad shelf of the Florida plateau that lay in the Gulf emerged, doubling the width of the peninsula. During the periodic glacial retreats there were warm intervals, and the sea, released again, poured over the plateau, leaving only a few thin strands of dry land. Seven well-defined marine terraces were left behind to mark successive invasions of the sea at 270, 215, 170, 100, 42, and 25 feet above its present level. South Florida emerged only a hundred thousand to seventy-five thousand years ago, receiving its final lamination of limestone, a formation called Miami oolite, in the high seas of the third interglacial period. In the final ice age, ten thousand years ago, the sea retreated again, leaving Florida Bay, at the southern tip of the peninsula, empty. Across these flats, at some point, a herd of white-tailed deer wandered over to the Keys, only to be stranded there when the sea rose again. Today a race of stunted Key deer, about the size of goats, survives.

The finished product, Florida today, is dead flat in most places, as you would expect a shallow sea floor to be, and it still communicates with the sea along the one thousand one hundred and fifty miles of its shoreline. Everywhere there are reminders of the past. In the Kissimmee Valley, for example, fifty miles from either coast, you can stir the sand with your foot and kick up sea shells that are twenty million years old. A much more important reminder of the geological past is the Floridan Aquifer. Lying in a thick bed above the granite and sandstone basement of the Florida plateau thousands of feet down are layers of a highly porous "honeycomb" limestone, holding one of the most abundant reservoirs of fresh water in the world. The limestone is much like a sponge, soaking up more water than it allows to travel over its surface, and of the fifty-three inches of rain that Florida gets in a normal year, only fourteen, or about a quarter of the water, runs off in streams and rivers. The rest percolates down through fissures, crevices, and conduits into vast, water-worn underground chambers.

This system underlies the entire state at various depths and gives the peninsula a distinct hydrologic character. Sometimes a creek will be running along smoothly when it will suddenly slip into the ground, never to be seen again, unless it can be related to the equally unexpected emergence of another creek in a basin miles away, or to the bubbling up of a limpid spring, hundreds of which are released from the Aquifer by natural artesian pressure.

The Aquifer presents some problems too. When water travels so quickly and freely underground, there is not always time or sufficient thicknesses of sand and gravel to strain out its impurities before it is brought up again for consumption. Most of Florida, therefore, is actually unsuitable for extensive ground sewage disposal—a factor which many of the developers in the state have overlooked. The results of this oversight can be jolting, as in March, 1973, when the citizens of Miami were asked to boil their water before drinking it, to avoid possible contamination coming from their own waste.

Sometimes the roof of an underground cavern in the Aquifer will collapse, making a thunderous noise and leaving a gaping hole in the ground known as a "sink." This kind of unsettling event is fairly common in the Central Highlands, especially in the "dead-zone karst" country, where there are hollow chambers above the present surface of the ground water. In recent years the ground has caved in on a Buick, a mule pulling a plow, and a lawn on the University of Florida campus at Gainesville. One of the most imposing sinks in the state is the Devil's Millhopper, just north of Gainesville on the edge of a great forest. On a sunny afternoon in February I stood at the edge of this great crater, looking down. The sink is a hundred feet or so to the bottom and four hundred feet to the other side, where a radio mast supported by cables stands high over the mature pines and hardwoods that make up the San Felasco Hammock. The sink has been there certainly as long as the white man has, and probably longer, and around its rim great beeches, magnolias, lo-blolly pines, live oaks, and sweet gums pour their thick trunks upward, uninterrupted by limbs for most of their height. A long-haired boy in a checkered shirt was swinging out over the edge of the sink on a wild grapevine that hung from one of the big trees while three of his friends sat passing a joint of marijuana back and forth. Other long-haired freaks were perched in small groups on various ledges and promontories, gazing on the scene.

I lowered myself down a nearly vertical path in the sink, clinging to roots and brittle limestone projections, examining the moist walls of corrugated yellow rock, the streaks of blue clay, the bristling ferns and palmettos. At the bottom the climate is completely different. Mosses and liverworts found nowhere else in Florida are there, and other plants more typical of North Carolina. Twelve springs spill down the walls of the sink, meeting at the bottom in a creek that glides across its gravel floor and then slips suddenly into a waterworn hole and disappears. The water is green and gives a greenish cast to the pebbles it travels over. I stooped down and tasted it from my cupped hand. Like most of the water in Florida, it is flat and chalky, charged with calcium carbonate and other minerals, and it is seventy-two degrees, the year-round temperature of all the ground water in the state. To make this cavity the water had eaten through roughly thirty-five million years' accumulation of limestone, down to the very first layers that were deposited on the metamorphic rocks of the ancient sunken Florida plateau. This earliest group of limestones, called the Ocala Formation, is rich in fossils, and the floor of the Devil's Millhopper is littered with them. I picked up handfuls of gravel from the creek bed and sifted through them. In no time at all I had found a manta-ray tooth with grooves like a file, and a thin shark's tooth with a deadly point, both about sixty-five million years old; some amorphous phosphitic pebbles; a sliver of bone, perhaps part of a manatee rib; a mastodon molar from Pleistocene glacier days; and a beer can, riddled with bullet holes, that had been there just long enough to acquire some rust. Above me, a little ball of midges, just hatched, tumbled around in the air and a Carolina wren hopped up the wall, apparently looking for a place to nest. I went up to the dark, slimy hole where the creek disappeared, swishing through brown foam, then falling what sounded like a considerable drop into the Floridan Aquifer.

While technically north of the tropics, most of the peninsula is subject to the tropical pattern of wet and dry seasons. The seasonal extremes, for those who must live with them, are in their own way as spectacular as the changes between winter and summer in the North. From the end of October, 1970, for example, to April, 1971, it rained only 2.05 inches at Miami International Airport, while on October 18, 1965, 25 inches fell on Fort Lauderdale in less than twenty-four hours. The wet season, or hydroperiod, is usually from June to October, when hot air masses sump up large quantities of seawater and dump them on the land. In the spring, when freshets are streaming down hillsides on the rest of the continent, Florida goes through its dry spell. The high fire season in the Ocala National Forest is from May to June. All the conditions are right: the forest is bone dry, there is a maximum of leaf litter on the forest floor, the needles of the sand pine exude an explosive varnish that is like turpentine, and a warm wind blows from the southwest. The fires are ignited by lightning, and when they get going, they can rip through the tops of the pines, or "crown," at sixty to eighty miles an hour. The last catastrophic fire in the Ocala Forest wiped out twenty thousand acres in several minutes.

In the spring of 1971, a combination of extreme lack of rain, water mismanagement, and overpopulation produced Florida's worst

SILVER METEORS PASS IN THE SCENIC HIGHLANDS OF FLORIDA

drought in modern times. There were fires in the Everglades unlike any in memory, not just the lightning strikes that burn off the saw grass, scorch the shells of box turtles, and go out when they get down to the moist peat topsoil. That spring was so dry that there wasn't any water in the peat, so the peat caught fire and burned for weeks, right down to bedrock. By the time the flames were put out they had destroyed thirty-six thousand acres of Everglades and come within twelve miles of downtown Miami. And fire was not the only problem. By May, the Gold Coast was on water rations. This megalopolis, extending from Palm Beach to Miami and including twenty-seven adjoining cities, depends for water on Lake Okeechobee and on seepage from the lake into another subterranean reservoir, the Biscayne Aquifer. Miami alone uses a hundred and fifty million gallons a day. But, unfortunately, the previous summer most of the water in the lake had been rushed out to sea through canals in order to avert floods. To top everything, much of the tourist season on the Gold Coast, during which the population doubles, coincides with the dry season, and that year the problems were acute. Just as things were getting really critical, however, the summer rains came.

As the sea drew back during the glacial periods, plants began to colonize the peninsula. Seeds of gumbo-limbo, mahogany, and other species with salt-resistant cases drifted up from the Caribbean basin or were brought in by birds. Southern oaks, hickories, and other woodland trees spread down from the coastal plains and eventually formed associations with the Caribbean trees in hardwood stands called "hammocks." Seedlings of red, white, and black mangrove floated over from Africa on the equatorial current, and a heavy mangrove screen sprouted along the coasts. Gradually the peninsula was covered with an intricate mosaic of plant communities—seventeen distinct ones in all. The distinctions are often blurred in the areas where one community is in the process of absorbing another.

In each place the presence or absence of fire and water have helped determine what plants should grow there. The low, wet basins favor fresh-water marshes with tall grasses, sedges, rushes, and scattered cattails and buttonwoods. The greatest marsh is the Everglades, dominated by saw grass, a three-edged sedge with sharp barbs that will tear your skin if you run your finger quickly up a blade of it. But men have upset the regime of water in the Everglades with flood control and reclamation projects, and much of the marsh is turning into a wet prairie, whose shorter grasses and sedges prefer the drier conditions and the new hydroperiod, shorter by two months, which the drainage canals impose. Not only the Everglades, but many lakes in Florida are turning into wet prairies as people make greater demands on the water supply. Willows and button-bushes are coming into the decadent lakes that have been wet prairies for some time. It is interesting to consider how these shrubs got there—how the water was drawn off to give elderly people on the coast the consolation of flowers; to cool the air-conditioners that now do the job of fans and fly swatters in most places; to grow citrus to be shipped north in refrigerator cars; to be used in mining phosphate. Given time, these wet prairies will dry out further and be invaded by the next community in the succession, the swamps.

You can see in many places little swamps standing in high, dry prairies: dome-shaped islands of bald cypress whose limbs bristle with air plants that look like pineapple tops and live on rain and dust. Actually, these swamps are not islands at all, but clay-lined bowls, which hold water. There are many kinds of swamps. Some have water tupelo standing in them; others are inhabited by the titi tree. There are "silver swamps" of loblolly bay, the silver undersides of whose leaves turn up in the breezes that come before rain.

In time, a swamp will dry out too, and the soil will become thick and rich enough to support a hammock, and then the succession will be complete, because hammocks are the climax growth in Florida.

Often, the dark moist verdure of a hammock is bordered by the comparative desert of a pine flatwoods. Sixty percent of the state is flatwoods—dry, open forest with saw palmettos and numerous herbs and shrubs in the understory, and the wispy plumes of slash, long-leaf, or pond pine in the canopy. Until recently, fire kept this plant community in balance. Every so often, during the dry season, wild fire would rage through, virtually unchecked, cleaning out the shrubs and leaves in the understory and making room for wildflowers to bloom in the spring. But men have upset the regime of fire in the flatwoods, and the periodic cleaning-out no longer occurs. Given time, the shrubs will choke out the pine, and the flatwoods too will eventually grow to be hammocks.

From about the town of Frostproof halfway down the peninsula, cabbage palms begin to multiply as you head south in the prairies, giving the scenery a tropical look. There begins to be a general profusion of wildlife, the likes of which is found nowhere else in the country. As George M. Barbour observed in the 1880s in a book called *Florida for Tourists, Invalids, and Settlers*, "the woods, fields, air, lakes, bays, and rivers are filled with fur, fin, and feather, flesh and fowl, oysters, turtles, and fruits." It is not unusual to be driving along at a leisurely speed late in the day past a billboard that says, THIS IS GOD'S COUNTRY. DON'T DRIVE THROUGH IT LIKE HELL, and to be suddenly overtaken by a large flock of glossy ibises which are following one of the highways that shoot down the lower half of the peninsula. You step on the gas and keep up with them for several miles until they veer off in one body and sail over to a drainage impoundment, joining assorted herons, egrets, and white ibises. Out on the water shearwaters are skimming the glassy surface, and pintails and coots are resting. The glossies wade around, feeding in silence, while meadowlarks whistle from hidden positions in the prairie.

Not all the vegetation that grows so exuberantly in Florida is appreciated. The state's chief weed is water hyacinth, *Eichornia crassipes,* which escaped from a lady's fish pond in 1884 and now infests approximately eighty thousand acres of the state's four-thousand-square-mile fresh-water surface. You see vast colonies of this noxious aquatic floating in many of Florida's thirty thousand lakes. It has heart-shaped leaves, a striking purple flower with an orange-centered bluish blotch on the uppermost petal, an inflated stalk, and a free-floating root system which extends for several feet when you pick it up out of the water. In less than a century water hyacinth has managed to usurp the niches of the yellow water lily and several other native aquatics. It has no native enemies. It impedes navigation, snags the lines and propellers of fishermen, stops the flow of water, and sterilizes bottoms by cutting off submerged plants from sunlight. Furthermore, its minute seeds are of practically no value to wild life. On the other hand, hyacinths have become the home of several hundred animals: scuds, snails, fairy shrimps, larval dragonflies, and blind mosquitoes. They also consume some of the overload of nutrients in the lakes, many of which have been made eutrophic, or overenriched, by the citrus groves, sewage plants, and vacation homes that line their shores.

The Lay of the Land 29

WHISPERING PINES COURT, Ft. Pierce, Fla. Ideally Located In The Southland.

The state of Florida spends ten million dollars a year weeding out water hyacinths. Several agencies vie for the honor of eradicating them. The Game and Fish Commission takes care of the plants on the major rivers, lakes, large creeks, and streams. The Army Corps of Engineers, which is responsible for maintaining the waterways, keeps the upper St. Johns River clear for fuel barges and also removes the hyacinths on Lake Okeechobee. The Central and Southern Flood Control District polices the plants in its own drainage canals. The counties see to the smaller lakes, creeks, public canals, and county drainage ditches. In some counties prison gangs wade up to their armpits, pulling up hyacinths, but their contribution is negligible. And, finally, the private developers weed out the plants in their own canals.

There are two ways to get rid of *Eichornia crassipes*. You can spray it with 2–4–D, a rapidly degradable World War II defoliant which mimics the plant's growth hormones and makes the cells divide so rapidly that it expires. The trouble with this method is that the dead hyacinths sink to the bottom and smother it with a flatulent mat of rotting vegetation which contributes to the overenrichment of the water and turns it into a pea-green sludge, thus killing off bass and other fish which feed by sight. The big mechanical harvesters that operate from land or on barges do a more thorough job of eradication. Harvested *Eichornia crassipes* have a number of uses. Chopped up and sprayed with molasses, they make good cattle feed. They are used to replenish the reclaimed muck soil south of Lake Okeechobee, which is gradually disintegrating on contact with the air and blowing away. Hyacinths also make good fertilizer and mulch, and can even be made into paperboard.

Most of the Florida where people choose to be has undergone major surgery several times, and the feverish events of the last few decades have been as important in determining the face of the land as the millennial processes that brought it into being—especially along the coasts. Although the peninsula was one of the first parts of the New World known to European man, it was a forbidding region, underwater half the time. Before it was any good to him, it had to be essentially destroyed. It wasn't till four hundred years after its discovery that men developed motives and machinery for reclaiming the peninsula. And the men who tackled the problem seem to have been more interested in getting rich than in establishing a long-term relationship with the terrain. Much of the development was based on misinformation and on inappropriate ideas imported from the sturdier landscapes of the North. The spirit of the times did not give rise to austere, thoughtfully laid-out villages like the ones that still survive in New England. It was more the way Frederick Lewis Allen catches it in *Only Yesterday:*

> The shirt-sleeved crowds hurrying to and fro under the widely advertised Florida sun talked of binders and options and hundred-thousand-dollar profits; the city fathers had been forced to pass an ordinance forbidding the sale of property in the street, or even the showing of a map, to prevent inordinate traffic congestion. The warm air vibrated with the clutter of riveters, for the steel skeletons of skyscrapers were rising to give Miami a skyline appropriate to its metropolitan destiny. Motor buses roared down Flagler Street, carrying "prospects" on free trips to watch dredges and steam shovels converting the outlying mangrove swamps and the sandbars of the Bay of Biscayne into gorgeous Venetian cities for the American homemakers and pleasure-seekers of the future.

The civilization that ensued can hardly be said to have followed any more of a master plan than do the weeds that find their way into a vacant lot. There seems to be a sort of natural succession to the buildings, though. Mobile homes, for instance, are replaced by Jimmy Walters prefabricated shell homes as the humanity in an area becomes denser and more established. Rustic Alamo gas station–bar–general stores tend to give way to half-Tudor shopping plazas with five-acre parking lots. Gracious old suburbs are absorbed by the expanding metropolis. The shell-encrusted Moorish mansions of Palm Beach have had their day; few can afford to play the games that were once played in them. The white stucco hotels of Miami Beach are on their last legs too. They have been emptied by jumbo jets that fly to cheaper, more appetizing tropical resorts in the Caribbean and displaced by snazzy new condominiums. Coming in are more jai alai stadiums, dog tracks, snake farms, juicer plants, junior colleges, pet cemeteries, utopian retirement communities, health clubs, drive-ins, car dealerships, funeral chapels, barbecue pits, hamburger franchises, and amusement parks, or, as the colossal ones are called, theme parks.

The current fantasy in central Florida is Disney World. As a result of the opening in 1971 of "the most gargantuan vacation enterprise ever devised," Orange County, where it is located, is experiencing the greatest population explosion in American history. In its first year, when Disney World had more visitors than the entire population of Florida, the county had to spend five million dollars for bigger roads and two and a half million dollars for expanded services, including an increase of three hundred thousand dollars in the welfare budget to deal with the drifters who showed up looking for jobs in the Magic Kingdom. During this time the Salvation Army in Orlando handled sixty thousand cases, robberies in the city went up seventy-one percent from the year before, and arrests for drugs and prostitution were up forty-five percent. A million dollars was spent for additional law-enforcement personnel. Since the time that Disney representatives secretly acquired the site for an average of a hundred and eighty-five dollars an acre, businesses have paid up to three hundred thousand an acre for lots near the park, while the land in Sebring, a sleepy town ninety miles south, has gone up to twenty-five thousand an acre. Taxes in Orange County have become "out of sight" for the retirees on small fixed incomes who make up twenty-one percent of the county. Many have sold their spreads and moved on to cheaper, quieter parts. It seems like the boom twenties all over again in central Florida.

"The sun of Florida's destiny has arisen, and only the malicious and the short-sighted contend or believe that it will ever set." So wrote John W. Martin, who was governor of Florida in 1925. The ironic part of it is that, of all the states, Florida is probably the most fragile. Yet, sadly, it is the one which the American way of life has attacked with, perhaps, the greatest vehemence.

That Long Vacation

In recent years impressive numbers of elderly folks have been descending on the state of Florida. According to one source, at least three thousand one hundred more Americans past the age of sixty-five arrive every week. Their new home may be a cinderblock ranchhouse on a former ranch or reclaimed wetland, or on one of the "fingerfills," the spits of dredged seabottom that perforate the coast in neat rows. It may be a twenty-room mansion in Palm Beach, a three-room Jimmy Walters shell home, that can be assembled anywhere in three weeks, or a single room in a rest home. If they are members of the Loyal Order of the Moose, they are eligible to live at Moosehaven, and if they are Lutheran, there is a place for them at the East Ridge Lutheran Village at Perrine. Many move into adult mobile-home communities.

Ever since Ponce de León came to a land that was "full of flowers" to investigate rumors about a fountain of youth, Florida has been thought of as a place where you can take out a new lease on life. By the end of the nineteenth century, it was already an established mecca for the old and the infirm. But it wasn't until World War II that the migration began to take on tidal proportions, as elderly people from all over the country were ordered south by their doctors, enticed by "swamp peddlers" to buy lots in Florida sight unseen, driven out of their home towns by taxes they couldn't afford, and abandoned by their kin in the peculiar way we seem to do it here. Lately their ranks have been swollen by the first wave of retirees to benefit from the big pension boosts of the fifties. Today more than one Floridian in four receives social security and is spending it on "that long vacation," or what is billed as "the rest of your life" by a hotel in Miami Beach, where signs forbid you to touch the knobs of the television in the lobby or to spit in the men's room sink.

The facts are lavishly publicized: a child born in Florida has a life expectancy eighteen months higher than the national average, and a retiree between sixty and seventy can expect to live a full year longer if he chooses to spend his "harvest years" in Florida. It seems to be the healthiest place in the world. Death from the diseases of old age—heart disease, TB, arteriosclerosis, and diabetes—are all well below the figures for the nation as a whole, and until the great migrations from the north, the cancer rate was lower too. The reason for this, it's widely held, has something to do with the unusually intense ultraviolet rays with which the state is blessed. It is all explained in the chapter on sunshine in a low-income retirement guide called *Norman Ford's Florida*, which I ordered through an ad in the *Farmer's Almanac*:

> Modern day climatologists are almost unanimous that the chief factor in determining the value of a climate lies in the average intensity of its

ultra-violet light. Ultra-violet waves are, of course, those light rays having the shortest wave length. Owing to this fact, they are quickly dispersed by dust and particles held in suspension in the air. When allowed to reach the earth in full measure, their effect is strongly aseptic which may well account for the prevalence of pneumonia and other germs in cities where dust and smog prevent ingress of ultra-violet light. Perfectly free from the dust or smog, the wine-clear air of Florida allows a maximum of ultra-violet rays to reach its sandy surface.

Perhaps the best living proof of the power of ultraviolet light is Charley Smith, at a hundred and thirty the oldest man in Florida. Smith, with whom I chatted one day, has spent the last sixty years in Bartow and lucidly recalls the morning in Liberia a hundred and eighteen years ago when he was watching his mother make sausages and a man named Legree shanghaied him and sold him into slavery to a Texan named Charley Smith. Smith sits pretty much all day on a bench in front of his candy store, absorbing prodigious quantities of ultraviolet light. He's not so sure about the connection with longevity one way or the other.

The first thing you have to do to get a new lease on life, according to Norman Ford, is to clear out of your home town. There's no sense staying in the place where you'd been in your prime, slowly fading out of the picture and becoming a shadow of your former self. Not when you can pack up and head for Florida, where thousands of people like yourself are living on small but adequate fixed incomes and participating in the seventy-five recreations most enjoyed by retirees: softball, gardening, hunting, shelling, dancing, golf, diamond ball, lawn bowling, beachcombing, tennis, bicycling, quoits, volleyball, square dancing, badminton, carpentry, archery, needlecraft, bridge, sailing, canoeing, and pedal boating, to name but a

The Famous Green Benches at St. Petersburg, Florida

P-187

few. You can move into a "planned community for happy, ambulatory adults," like the Del Webb Corporation's Sun City Center, south of Tampa, where thirty-five hundred oldsters tool around in golf carts, get married at ninety, and take part in a new life style called "renewment," which offers constant companionship in a nonstop program of activities. "I saw one man slump over while he was square dancing," one resident recalled. "He just went down with a great big smile on his face. I can't think of a better way to go."

There are, of course, all sorts of retirees. The rich ones, who have time and money and believe in keeping things the way they are, often become active conservationists. Sarasota County, which has a large number of well-to-do elderly people, has repeatedly voted down the propositions of developers, and is reputed to be one of the most conservation-minded places in the country. The average working-class retiree, however, is completely absorbed in his parcel of paradise. During the day he can usually be found outside, hosing down his Studebaker, fussing with his frangipani, or spraying his lawn with dexterous manipulations of the nozzle. At night he visits or stays home and faces the grim realities of pollution, crime, overcrowding, drugs, unemployment, and ghettoes in the paper or on the six o'clock news. Many retirement compounds are completely self-contained. Their inhabitants are often quite happy. Extreme retirement doesn't agree with everyone, of course. There are always some old folks who, cut off from children, old friends, and the swim of things, and aggravated by the mosquitoes in summer, finally pack up and go home north.

Surprisingly, the most senescent city in the state is not St. Petersburg, with its famous green benches installed throughout the town so the oldsters can watch the passing scene. With a whopping forty-nine percent of its population over sixty-five, the distinction belongs to Miami Beach. In fact, as far as the publicity people of the Beach are concerned, there are so many elderly that they dampen the town and freak out the young couples who come to Florida to swing. In 1970 the average annual occupancy rate for Miami Beach's hotels was sixty-five percent, down from sixty-nine percent five years earlier. This was attributed partly to the depressing droves of old folks. So since that time the Beach's p.r. machinery has been frantically trying to "think young," sponsoring mass marriages, rock concerts, and other events that might attract the cheerful sight of youth.

One muggy afternoon I decided to take a tour of the *dolce vita* in Miami Beach. Breezing along between the white walls of stucco hotels, "condos" (condominiums), and efficiency apartments, I became part of a motorcade headed by a man in track shorts who was running down Route A–1–A, the town's congested main drag, with a torch in one hand to proclaim the opening of a new health club. Behind him two peaches sat up in the back seat of a pink Eldorado convertible and waved. Pretty soon, though, the people behind them became ticked off at having to slow down to the pace of a running man, and, honking their horns, filled the sunflooded canyon with their klaxon bleating until the runner and his party ducked up a side street. Traffic flowed normally again only to pull over minutes later as a red rescue van wailed by. The mobile rescue squads of Miami Beach are said to be the only ones in the country that carry doctors, and as a result seven out of ten victims of cardiac arrest here make it to the hospital alive, whereas in the nation at large only one in five hold on that long.

While attempting to park in front of the Hotel Fontainebleau I backed into the fender of the car behind me. The driver of the dented vehicle, a white-haired cabbie retired from the New York rat race and now waiting to be hailed by some lady in pastel mink, let out a string of expletives that would have made a Times Square hustler blush. He finally agreed to "straighten it out for a fin."

On Ocean Drive the beach was lined with seedy whitewashed hotels in front of which rows of elderly women were sitting in deck chairs, stockings rolled down to their ankles, grimacing under white "nose-savers." Frequently they would get up to re-oil themselves. Between the hotels and the beach was a small park lined with palms and protected by numerous CURB YOUR DOG signs. A rabbinical-looking individual hurried past a bevy of peaches who were sitting on the beach with arms propped behind them watching an ocean-liner called the *Emerald Seas* pull out of the harbor. An old gentleman was sitting in the surf, letting the rollers break gently on his body and staring at his toes. A miniature couple, the man in a dark suit with huge lapels and the woman deeply shaded by a lavender hat, shakily approached a green bench. The man ran his hand over the wooden bars, showed it to the woman, and after some deliberation they laid down some newspaper and sat down together. A musclebound bronzed Apollo, bulging obscenely, as if to burst his tight striped swimsuit, pranced by along the edge of the foam.

As I poked around looking for trouble, a sidewalk huckster hucksterd me into the Roxy Theater for the two o'clock perfor-mance of *Sepia-72*, an all-black burlesque show. The first three rows were filled with retirees direct from New York City's garment dis-trict—men smoking fat cigars, wearing Bermuda shorts, knee socks, caps, and gold fobs connecting their "Loyal Service" watches to the buttonholes of Truman shirts. A band of white-haired black musicians was sitting at the rear of the smoke-filled stage, manning the trumpet, drums, saxophone, and electric guitar. As they played slow, sultry numbers like "Misty," "Summertime," "My Mama Done Told Me," and "That Old Black Magic," the girls came on one by one and strutted their stuff: Miss Lolita ("the Body"), Miss Maria, Miss Mustang Sally, Miss Zi Zi, Miss Mary Ford. First their angelic see-through white robes fell to the floor, then their sequined sheaths, then their spangled cups, then, singing to themselves as they danced, they went all the way. The star of the show was Lady Ernestine, the Dark Angel of the Runway. She came out with a fan and a platinum-blond wig and slowly worked down to a black G-string, and then, her eyes sparkling wickedly, she peeled it off and ran her fingers over the only body she had. The retirees sat back in their chairs and sent up appreciative billows of smoke. Then a master of ceremonies came out and said, "All these lovely ladies taking all their clothes off, they should be locked up . . . they should be locked up . . . in my motel room with me."

I spent several hours plunging north through the sunbaked honky-tonk of the Gold Coast finally arriving at a tiny island named by its original Indian inhabitants Hypoluxo. No Indians now, but Joe Namath is alleged to have a secret pad here, and on the northern part of the island is a house that once belonged to the brother of Oscar Hammerstein; it's where most of the lyrics for *South Pacific* were written. The house is now in the hands of a Boston Irishman named Patrick T. Cecere and his wife Jean. Pat and I know each other because he owns two houses in Cambridge, Massachusetts, and I rented an apartment in one of them for several months.

The previous November, while working as a hostess in a motel

SCENE ON OCKLAWAHA RIVER

in Lexington, Massachusetts, Jean had almost collapsed from nervous tension, and they had both decided they had had enough of the "goddamn strain of the city," and had moved to Hypoluxo, even though Pat had five years to go at the Western Electric Company in Waltham. Pat had told me to drop in and see him any time I was in Florida, but I think he was a little startled when I actually appeared at the door. He was wearing a light blue boating cap that had FLORIDA stitched across the front, and there was a new brightness to his smile and a lightness to his step now that he was free from the hassles of being a landlord. "You can't be a good guy and be in business," he told me.

"I was going day and night," he said. "All my life I'd never had a vacation. So this is really something for me." He stripped off his warmup jacket to reveal his tan and the site of his vanished pot belly. "I been so goddamn busy down here, Alex, the day don't seem long enough." There was a twenty-three-foot powerboat he had gotten "tied up in," which was over at the marina having new gaskets installed. There were navigation courses at night, and free lessons that came with the organ he had just bought. There was a kidney-shaped pool in the backyard for whenever he felt like cooling off, and trees that required attention: banyan, mango, avocado, kumquat, powderpuff, orchid, and a huge strangler fig that had wrapped a cabbage palm in its deadly embrace and all but deprived it of light. "The roots travel like hell," he said. "Here's one." He kicked a root that had surfaced briefly on the lawn. "I broke my shovel on this bastard."

The backyard was right on the water, and waves made by boats traveling up the Intracoastal Waterway gently laved the crushed shells of Pat's private beach. About fifty feet out there was a metal stake which his son had helped him drive in to moor his boat. "You could start walking here and by the time you get to that stake you wouldn't be over your knees." He picked up a line that went out to a pulley on the stake and explained that it was for running the boat in at high tide.

"Of course the island here is just loaded with raccoons," he went on as we entered a sun porch which had aluminum windows cranked open on three sides, a terrazzo tile floor, a bar with two tilted anchors on its veneer paneling, an enormous color television, and a fish tank and which was called a Florida room. We went through the house, looked in on the missus in the kitchen, and came out near a two-car garage containing the same maroon Continental Pat had driven around Cambridge, now with plates which said SUNSHINE STATE— ARRIVE ALIVE—FLORIDA. As we shook hands, Rocky, Pat's Chinese pug, which had paid no attention to me up to that moment, growled. "This house set me back sixty-five grand," he told me, "but I wouldn't take a hundred for it."

The next day I visited a different retirement proposition, Hobe Sound on Jupiter Inlet, an encapsulated community of elderly WASP millionaires, where soothing groves of Australian pine line the beach, and huge green turtles still come out of the sea and bury their eggs in the sands of the long barrier island. The continental shelf is practically nonexistent here, and you can stand on the beach and see the deep blue intensity of the Gulf Stream just offshore, where the green shallows break off. I spent a placid Sunday morning with Archibald Roosevelt, Theodore's octogenarian son, waiting to see a painted bunting come to the feeder on his terrace. Like his father, he has a strong feeling for the natural world, and our conversation was about birds, the enormous flocks of robins that come down to Florida and get drunk on holly, the saw-whet owl that "bored me to death last night," the Key deer who have developed a taste for cigarette butts and are often run over by campers, the alligator who lives in a water hazard on the golf course and has pulled several dogs under. Hobe Sound is "done with money," and resembles some parts of the North Shore of Long Island more than anywhere in Florida. The houses are the same gracious brick manors surrounded by rhododendrons and other broad-leafed shrubs. The same people migrate seasonally between the two places and do the same things, I am told: swat golf and tennis balls by day and party at night. On the way out of Hobe Sound I stopped at the post office and was reprimanded by a distinguished white-haired gentleman in a blazer who said that it was "awfully inconsiderate" of me to have left my car in his space.

Sarasota, across the peninsula, is the retirement capital of the circus world. When an aging acrobat or sword swallower, down wintering with the troupe, doesn't feel like traveling any more, he simply stays behind in Sarasota. Members of the same troupe, with a lifetime on the road in common, often retire together. One community like that is the Giant's Camp, twenty miles or so north of Sarasota. It was run by Al Tomani, who dressed in cowboy suits and was the next-to-tallest man in the world until his death eight years ago. "The one in Ioway—I forget his name—he was the tallest," said a man who weighed five hundred pounds easily and was standing on a dock with a beer next to two freshly caught five-foot tarpon. The camp is now run by the Giant's widow, who was born without legs. Together they had been "The World's Strangest Couple" in the old Ringling Brothers and Barnum & Bailey sideshow until it broke up in Wolfsbury, Pennsylvania, in 1938. The show had also featured Eko and Iko, "ministers from Dahomey"—two blond Ethiopians who were born with what was advertised as sheeps' wool on their heads; a Hawaiian band; a tattooed girl; and the Doll Family, a family of midgets, one of whom, Harry Doll, wore tails, parted his hair down the middle, and was a familiar figure in the movies of the forties.

I walked between two huge black rubber cowboy boots up to some old trailers of riveted sheet metal and knocked on one. Candy Shelton, the former sideshow manager, came to the door in his undershirt. He was cooking himself some lima beans, but said he was always glad to talk to somebody about old times. I helped him get a trunk out of the closet that was filled with yellowed clippings, snapshots, and circus route books. "You people your age never seen a real circus. It was a wonderful institution. It's a darn shame they don't exist any more." We looked at the 1937 route book: 1,608 people in the show, 15,427 miles traveled, 404 performances given, one lost. Wednesday, August 11, Oshkosh, Wisconsin: "Weather turned cooler and a real good day's business was the result."

I took Candy's greetings to the Doll family, who live in Sarasota in a cozy bungalow that is the size of a large dollhouse, built a few feet off the ground, and surrounded with poincianas, birds of paradise, and other lovely flowers. One of the two surviving midgets, Miss Doll, came to the door, but did not ask me in. She said they had left the circus and just wanted to be left alone. "We quit the gaggle. We done that all our lives."

Christmas in the Midlands

I woke up in the back seat of my convertible, safely stashed between two manicured rows of yellow pine in "The Forest of the Future" near Fort Meade. A mockingbird was singing his heart out on a telephone wire. Suddenly he left his perch and continued to pour out his song in midair, hovering and fluttering as if buoyed up by sheer elation. By the time he had settled down on top of a fencepost, I guess I understood why he had been elected the state bird by a vote of the schoolchildren of Florida. Out in a clearing a fallow cornfield covered over with hay gleamed in the sun, with a few broken stalks sticking through. A powerful stench rose into my nostrils from two flattened carcasses lying in a ditch, one of a beagle and the other of a smaller brown mutt, which someone must have picked up off the road and chucked over the fence.

Things in Florida flower and decay much faster than they do up North. Dead animals, left to the flies, the buzzards, and natural decay, return to the elements in a matter of days. "One thing

48

though," Norman Ford warns in his book on low-income Florida retirement, "that may cost you more in Florida is your refrigerator. You'll need a large one because more food must be stored in it than is customary in the North. Fruit, for example, that would keep sweet several days in the North can rot overnight during the Florida summer." It's been suggested more than once that if man's efforts to subdue Florida were relaxed for a generation most of the state would become primeval again. In evidence of this, as I drove through Polk County, I went by mounds of flame vine smothering the buildings of a gracious old Jackson-style farm that had been abandoned with the passing of that way of life and had already rotted beyond repair. And the fields around were overgrown with daisies, just waiting to be staked out in lots and turned into another Silver Springs Shores.

Little is left of the civilizations that once inhabited Florida. None of them mastered the wetness, the riotous growth, and the rapid decay. First the Caloosa Indians, with their poisoned darts and penis sheaths, and their elaborate kingfisher and alligator cults; there were about thirty thousand of them, but nothing remains to remind us they were here except for the great mounds of shells left from their generations of seafood dinners. The Spanish conquerors of the Caloosas arrived in numbers and with great plans but found little solid rock to build with except for coquina, the lithified shell mash which they used at the settlement of St. Augustine. They were displaced too and practically the only physical evidence of their having been there at all is the contribution they made to the state's gene pool—the occasional raven-haired coed strolling through the University of Florida campus at Gainesville.

As you drive inland from the coast, the high rises and phantasmagoric strips of the New Florida give way to scenes from the vanishing rural South: shacks with junk and garbage strewn around them, wash hanging out to dry; people eyeballing your New York plates suspiciously; Spanish moss swaying from trees and telephone lines in wide arcs shaped by the breeze; an old cracker collecting bottles in a gunnysack; a pretty young thing who couldn't be more than thirteen, walking along barefoot, a cigarette in her hand, looking up at you with sultry eyes; an old fellow peddling slowly with a bunch of bananas draped over the handlebars; a crone in a woolen hat bringing her groceries home in a little red wagon; a black woman with a red kerchief round her head, a bucket in one hand and two long cane poles in the other, walking deliberately with her head down, singing to herself; a profusion of trailers and gospel meetings; fundamentalist churches black and white; car cemeteries; flea markets; thrift shops; and signs offering to buy, sell, or trade anything, you name it.

Six miles south of the orange-juice plant in Umatilla, I pulled off Highway 33 to check the view from a fire tower. It is a goodly tower, one hundred and twenty feet tall and commanding a view of a hundred and fifty thousand acres on a good day, a bird's eye view of the Midlands: orange groves, pine flatwoods, and the lacy pattern of innumerable shallow lakes as far as I could see. As I was coming down an old man stepped out of the house below the tower and asked if I'd ever picked an orange before. "No, sir," I replied.

"I saw Roy Rogers on television last night," said the man, whose name was Vadam White. "He said the first time he was in Florida he damn near was arrested 'cause he saw all those orange trees and he just had to go out and pick them." Five years ago Mr. White sold his farm in Peachtree, Georgia, and bought this spread. He is sixty-six now and lives here with a wife who "gets aggravated by the gnats," a son about eleven, half a dozen hens, two chihuahuas named Trixy and Tiny, and a cow he was fattening for the Lake County Fair. He took me into his grove, gave me a paper bag, and told me to "he'p yo'sef." I filled it with navels, temples, bloods, and honey-murcott tangelos. Their skins were green, yellow, and black, and they didn't look anything like supermarket oranges, which are soaked in a waxy dye and stamped FLORIDA. We sat on the tailgate of his Chevrolet Cheyenne sucking citrus and shooting the breeze. "I was only in New York but once and I never want to go back," he said. "Me and my buddy drove up to Virginia to visit the World's Fair. That was back in thirty-nine. I had athletic feet at the time and by end of the day it looked like you could peel my toes right off." A car pulled up in front of the tower, and Mr. White suddenly fell silent, watching. A man got out of the car, took his jacket off, threw it in the back seat, got back in, and drove off. "I like to enjoy myself," Mr. White resumed, once things had settled down again, "take the dogs out for a rabbit chase, walk around in my bathing suit." A shiny hearse went by, then a battered gray bus, owned and operated by Bill "Runt" Cumbee, which was returning fruit pickers to Haines City.

Behind the orange grove there was a lake and Mr. White said I could camp there for the night if I felt like it. I said thanks, I was planning to make Lakeland by nightfall, but I sure would like to take a look if that was o.k. It was, so I walked back through his grove, past a big box turtle struggling through the loose gray sand; down a road that went on a raised dike across a cypress swamp; past a small island with a tree decked in Spanish moss like a pavilion, atop which a kingfisher was chuckling infectiously. A swarm of flies was feasting

on the thick yellow belly of a moccasin that floated dead in the dark water. Big green darners and black-winged damselflies were visiting the flowers. I was startled to see a brown thrasher, a bird I associate with the thickets of New England, scratching under the palmettos. He could have been a migrant or a resident: some thrashers live in the northern half of Florida all year round; others come down only for the winter. Consorting with the bird were tropical butterflies I'd never seen before, queens and zebras, skipping in the sunshine. The road continued across a dry prairie into a grove of crooked young oaks and stopped at the edge of a lake, where a big white camper was parked.

The door was open, and I could see a woman inside sitting alone at a table rolling dice. Outside, flames danced in a barbecue grill, and a man stood in a boat on the lake, casting a bass plug toward the shore. "Okay, stick 'em up"—from behind me a voice that had not yet changed. I raised my hands and turned to see who had the drop on me, and found a boy squinting at me with a rubber dart feathered in a bow and drawn back to his cheek. "Wanna see a hole I found?" he asked, instead of letting it fly. We looked all over the grove for the hole, but couldn't find it again. When I returned to Mr. White, he presented me with a grapefruit that was as big as a volleyball. I told him that whoever had named that lake Lake Perty hadn't been exaggerating. "Now don't forget the way," he said as I drove off.

It was Christmas Eve, and I was going to Lakeland to check out the thirty-foot plastic Christmas trees that are placed in each of the city's thirteen lakes during the holiday season. By the time I reached the Eastgate Lounge on the edge of town it was after dark, and the place was packed. A three-piece band (electric git-tar, bass git-tar, and a set of drums) was doing a country and western rock version of "The Midnight Special," and everybody was twisting with his gal. A woman with a two-foot-high purple permanent and wearing a red-checked work shirt and stretch slacks reeled along the wall to the ladies' room; and three men swaggered up from the parking lot, their shoulders hunched up and their arms stiff at their sides, as if ready for drawing six-guns. I pulled out *Norman Ford's Florida* and read the part about Lakeland: "Drinking water is sulfur-free," it said. "There is good t.v., a 450-bed hospital, and a well-stocked library. Southern College lends a cultural atmosphere." But Ford had nothing to say about the Eastgate Lounge, or about the Christmas Eve horror special—*Godzilla* and *Rodan*—at the drive-in, or about the Lakeland International Raceway, the Florida Citrus Mutual, the Lakeland Cash Feed Co., the Industrial Brush Co. and the Industrial Fence Co.; nor did he tell that Lakeland is the winter home of the Detroit Tigers, or that a large parade was recently held in the city by the Ku Klux Klan, led by the Grand Dragon himself.

I parked in the municipal parking lot and walked around the town square, peering into the darkened window of Johnny Reb's Early Bird Record Shop. One string of shops seemed to cater to the older set: a one-floor walkup with a sign in front of the stairs that said, BLOOD PRESSURE TAKEN INSIDE, $1.50; a natural-food store with such reading matter in the window as *Eat All Your Troubles Away;* a Christian Supply Center replete with inspirational leaflets ("Get a Higher Interest Rate on Your Heavenly Investment"); a card shop displaying lipstick containers that were actually something different: "Sheriff .'50—STOP ASSAULT INSTANTLY—up to fifty bursts—nontoxic but immediately effective."

A street led out to a lake in the middle of which stood one of the thirty-foot plastic evergreens surmounted by a blinking star. I walked all the way around the lake, meeting on the way a few senior citizens in the light of street lamps shaded this time of year with great red plastic sleighbells. The water caught the gleam of a half moon and held the shimmering reflections of the Hotel Terrace and the New Florida Hotel, two cracked and weathered pillars of prosperity built on the highest hill in town during the '24 land boom. Most of the rooms in the two hotels are now rented out to retirees on a long-term basis. In the Hotel Terrace, old men in fine suits out at the elbows were sleeping in the television room, hunched in dilapi-dated armchairs. A man ducked from one shadow to another, appar-ently not wanting to be seen. I went back to my car and fell asleep in the back seat, having dreams that were like sequences in an old gangster movie punctuated with the assorted whistles and bells of long trains that passed slowly through the square carrying pulpwood in open flatcars, citrus fruit in sealed aluminum cars, interspersed with older cars that were rusty red like southern clay. Early in the morning, Officer Tyus, on a motor scooter, tapped on the steamed-up window and ran a check on me and my convertible. Reassured by him that we weren't wanted, I dozed off again.

When I woke up the next time, the morning was half gone. An old duffer was sweeping the porch above Bob's Pawn Shop. I asked him where I could get a cup of coffee, but he didn't even look up. Stone deaf, I guess. There were signs of life at the bus-terminal café. I bought a Lakeland *Ledger* from the paper machine at the door, sat down in a phone booth, and started reading the Christmas editorial:

> The wheels quit spinning in this land of ours and over much of the world last night as tribute to the birth of a child. He grew into a

philosopher of sorts who uttered some great, great truths He was willing to die for.

We suppose the leading truth is that men should live like brothers.

This has proven to be a very difficult thing to do, since men come in various sizes and shapes and colors. If they're not out to make a buck, then they may wear long hair and listen to weird music . . .

The kids were home from school. Some were riding around the square in "muscle cars" and waving to friends. Two couples were cruising in a "Goat," which is what one calls one's GTO if one takes it seriously. They were followed by four couples crammed into a late model '55 modified Chevy coupé with jacked-up suspension and a glass muffler designed to sound like no muffler at all. In the phone booth next to mine a pockmarked blonde woman in hotpants with a little boy beside her was asking her husband if he felt like driving to the cemetery. "You know Jimmy's never been to my mother's grave."

I started thumbing through the yellow pages. While Lakeland isn't especially noted as a retirement haven, it does have forty-one mobile-home dealers and fifty-two trailer parks, many of which are undoubtedly occupied by senior citizens. Under "Retirement Homes" there were one retirement villa, one retirement ranch, and Rebecca's Rest Home:

"A Personalized Care Home"
AMBULATORY SENIOR CITIZENS
Lovely Residence—Good Food
Spacious Grounds—Field Trips
24 Hour Care
Complete Beauty and Grooming Care

I decided to bring the installation a little Christmas cheer. But first I pulled into Shorty's American service station, which was advertised by a big sign thrust up like a totem pole along Interstate 4. Shorty himself filled me up. He had sandy hair and came on real friendly. "Just two gallons short of the free jump rope," he said apologetically. Then he proceeded to pour in a quart of oil I didn't need, grinning and making conversation. "Becky's Rest Home? Sure I know where it is. Becky's a fine woman."

Becky turned out to be six years old. She is the daughter of Donna Langford, a handsome, energetic woman of thirty who had worked in a mental hospital as a physical therapist and recreation director before starting her own rest home. The home is like all the other cinderblock ranches on Dougherty Road, except instead of being a single-family residence it houses twelve elderly men and women who have been judged incompetent by their doctors, lawyers, and banks, and none of whose relatives are willing to care for them. One is from Canada, two are from New York, three from Chicago, three from Georgia, one from Alabama, one from Ohio, and one from Indiana. Each person pays three hundred to three hundred fifty dollars a month, depending on their medication needs, and lives an average of six months from the time of arrival. It is the kind of institution that one psychologist has described as "a practical method of storage till death." Are they happy? "No," Mrs. Langford said. "They'd rather die at home." She plans to begin work on a wing with twenty more rooms starting the first of the month.

"The majority are as senile as they'll ever get," she said. "They don't know if they've eaten, what time of day it is, or even their own names. But they never forget faces." They are cared for by seven girls working in two shifts and one full-time nurse named Linda who lives in an adjoining trailer. "They don't need a lavish place," Mrs. Langford went on. "Just good food and pleasant surroundings. First thing in the morning, before they come out, we do their hair and nails and put on their makeup if they were used to it. Most of them were, as young ladies. We try to stress their being human beings rather than vegetables. Yesterday we walked all over Tarpon Springs and took them out on a sponge boat. We try to get them out of the house once a week." In the house, they make things with ceramics and Hydrocal, a kind of plaster of Paris. The women regularly follow TV soap operas: *The Guiding Light, The Secret Storm, The Edge of Night, As the World Turns, Where the Heart Is, Love Is a Many Splendoured Thing, Search for Tomorrow,* and *The Love of Life.* Perry Mason is enjoyed by both sexes, and the men watch ball games. "They'll be out in a minute," Mrs. Langford said. "They're eating now."

After lunch the TV was turned on and we all sat in the living room. Four small women with lace-collared blouses and their hair in nets sat on a sofa babbling and eating chocolates they had received as Christmas presents. "We cracked open a bottle of champagne last night," Mrs. Langford said. "These people are religious, but they aren't hypocrites." Bertha Bernen, eighty-two, was singing an incoherent medley of tunes which included "Rudolph the Red-nosed Reindeer," "Engine, Engine Number Nine," and "Rock-a-bye Baby on the Tree Top." Beside her Theophila Kedzierski, sixty-three, was keeping up a constant stream of Polish and occasionally waving to imaginary friends who had passed by her front porch in Chicago, where she had been a dressmaker. Another woman was saying to nobody in particular across the room, "Smile while you're

FOUNTAIN OF YOUTH, ST. PETERSBURG, FLORIDA, "THE SUNSHINE CITY"——52

here. Baby's coming. Have a Merry Christmas." Meanwhile, on the
color TV Larry Czonka, running back for the Miami Dolphins, "the
human bowling ball," had just crashed through the nine-hundred-
forty-four-pound defensive line of the Baltimore Colts for a first
down. Molly Wilcen, seventy-six, of Chicago, said she had been here
"as long as I can remember. My husband died on the golf course.
I had to come here. That's the way it goes. My brother and sister
were here the other day. They live in that vicinity you were speaking
about and I didn't say it right. . . ." In the corner Denzil Downey,
sixty-three, whose shirt pocket bulged with three pens, a ruler, a
slide rule, and some envelopes, was making notes. "It's the darned-
est thing," he said. "You can string together plays for the Dolphins
on the TV, and the next day you can't remember your name." One
of the women got up, and Linda, the full-time nurse, who was
wearing one of the matching yellow warmup jackets that were given
to everybody on the staff for Christmas, caught her and started
waltzing her around the room. "It's not an unhappy place," Mrs.
Langford said. "We got a sense of humor. We're all nuts."

All that afternoon I played shuffleboard with George Haas, an
eighty-nine-year-old retired carpenter at the sumptuous home of the
Brotherhood of Carpenters and Joiners, in Gibsonia. Haas's back
wasn't too good, but his sense of humor was intact. As the plastic
discs slid over the smooth concrete, they sounded like icicles winged
across a frozen pond. With few exceptions, his would come to rest
precisely in the scoring zones, and mine would miss the grid completely or straddle a line, at which point Haas would slap his knee
with his faded blue boating cap and call out, "On the Line with
Considine," drawing his material from a TV news program that is
long gone.

The carpenters and joiners sure treat their retired brothers well. When they turn sixty-five and have paid their dues for thirty years, they get to live in this swell old stucco mansion that is built in the Moorish style and comes with two thousand acres, a golf course, a lake, a dairy and hog farm, and its own infirmary. There is a shop, too, but the old boys don't use it much; most of them probably don't care if they never see a two-by-four again. The brotherhood is a global organization, and even a few Czechs and Swedes live at the home.

Lined up in a cloister are about a hundred high-backed straw rockers, and maybe fifty of the home's two hundred and nine residents were sitting in them, watching a fine rain sift through the sunlight on Christmas afternoon. "Sitting and rocking while the world rolls by has many devotees," a brochure explained. "The spacious front porch offers ideal surroundings for such a pure pleasure." Charles Hewitt, ninety-one, from Salem, New Jersey, was watching a sparrow trying to muster up the courage to pick up some crumbs in front of his rocker. "Go ahead and eat. I'm not going to hurt you," he told the bird.

The shuffleboard courts are located in a grove of venerable old oaks and seventeen kinds of palms, through which you can see cars whizzing by on Route 98 and snow-white cattle egrets strutting around a pasture with a herd of Black Angus. Some of them perch right on the broad bovine backs. There is also a punk tree. "If you hit it with your cane it sounds dead," Haas said. He had come to the home in 1959, when his wife had died and there was nothing to keep him in Stamford, Connecticut. Stamford is just over the border from my home town of Bedford, New York, and I brought him up to date on all the new roads, office complexes, apartment houses, and department stores that had gone up since he'd last been there. I told him how there were traffic lights in downtown Stamford now, and everybody was marching in time with the red and the green. "I don't imagine I'd even recognize the place," he said.

Perhaps because we were surrounded by memorial benches, it was inevitable that we would get around to the subject of death. Twirling his shuffling dowl, Haas recalled the first house he and his brother, who had died the twenty-first of the previous month, had built together on Staten Island: "It was a brick veneer job. He says, Matty, he says, you do the brickwork and I'll do the carpentry and maybe we'll make a dollar or two." His brother never smoked or drank and belonged to the Masonic Order for twenty years.

"Well, at least you didn't get any minus," Haas said amicably as I turned in another scoreless round. I searched the remark for condescension, but he was beyond such things. As we edged our men back to the firing line, he communicated the peace of someone who had been released from ambition, contention, acquisitiveness, lust, and the other afflictions of youth. The thought that had bothered me at first, that this was probably the last game of shuffleboard we would play together, didn't seem so terrible to me in the face of such equanimity.

Some Rivers

Rising partly in the seven lakes of the Apopka chain and partly in an inaccessible depression west of these lakes called the Green Swamp, the Oklawaha River begins its journey to the sea running northward, parallel to the two coasts. At Silver Springs five hundred and fifty million gallons of ground water boil up into it daily, and the river becomes so clear that the catfish grazing on its sandy bottom thirty feet down seem within arm's reach. Then the river enters a dark hammock and is stained the color of tea by the leaves and roots of many hardwoods. Meandering extravagantly, it keeps running north till Orange Springs, where at last it makes a sharp right-angle bend and then heads east, merging, about eight miles below Lake George, with the St. Johns River and traveling with it to Jacksonville in the north and thence east and into the Atlantic Ocean. For the seventy miles of its existence it is one of the most enchanting stretches of river anywhere. Some scholars believe that Samuel Taylor Coleridge ignited a pipeful of opium shortly after reading about the Oklawaha in William Bartram's eighteenth-century account of his travels through Florida, and in the ensuing dream described it as Kubla Khan's river Alph, which ran, he said, "Through caverns measureless to man/Down to a sunless sea."

For years politicians and businessmen in Florida have had a different sort of dream: that of gouging across the peninsula a "waterway to prosperity," which would annually shuttle ninety million tons of chemicals, fertilizers, wood products, grain, petroleum, coal, steel, and other commodities between the Gulf and Atlantic coasts. The proposed route of this Cross-Florida Barge Canal, laid out in the thirties and modified in the fifties, would channelize roughly thirty miles of the Oklawaha and smaller segments of the Withlacoochee and the St. Johns rivers. In return, it would cut six hundred miles off the tankers' current sea voyage. It seems to many folks like a poor trade, especially since there is already a perfectly good waterway across Florida further down the peninsula: up the Caloosahatchee, across Lake Okeechobee, and out through the St. Lucie Canal. Its major problem is that it's for boats drawing only eight feet.

Work on the Cross-Florida Barge Canal was started in 1935 but stopped a year later, when hydrologists began to doubt if a sea-level canal could be dredged across the state without contaminating the Floridan Aquifer. On top of that, the U.S. Department of Commerce began to wonder about the canal's profitability. The project was revived in 1964 as the result of a more favorable cost-benefit study by the Army Corps of Engineers and an earlier campaign promise by John F. Kennedy. By 1968 a channel had been dredged through the shallow shelf of the Floridan plateau up to Yankeetown. There were locks and dams at Inglis and Eureka; there was a lock on the Oklawaha above where it joins the St. Johns; there were two bridge pilings, which had been put in in 1935 along Route 27 near Ocala; and there was a shallow fifty-five-hundred-acre reservoir called the Rodman Pool on the northern edge of the Ocala National Forest. The pool was created by the Corps of Engineers, who dammed the Oklawaha east of its right-angle bend and crushed hundreds of thousands of trees into the mud with a gigantic crawler-crusher retrieved from use in Vietnam. Somehow it didn't work. After a while the battered trees floated back to the surface, water hyacinths appeared and flourished, and the Rodman Pool, which the Corps had renamed Lake Oklawaha and hailed as a "fisherman's paradise," became a fetid quagmire.

In 1970 a group of concerned citizens founded the Florida Defenders of the Environment with the object of sabotaging the boondoggle, as they called the project. They prepared a study called the "Environmental Impact of the Cross-Florida Barge Canal With Special Emphasis on the Oklawaha Regional Ecosystem." This report attacked the canal from every angle, even pointing out errors in the Corps of Engineers' cost-benefit projection, and delivered as its verdict that the canal project was a "long-standing national disgrace." Largely as a result of the impression which this study made on his Council on Environmental Quality, President Nixon ordered a halt to the $185 million project in 1971. But it wasn't until February, 1973, that the Department of the Interior declared the Oklawaha a "wild and scenic river" and decided to buy up the canal authority's rights of way for about $13 million and to give them to the Ocala National Forest. Partly because of an irrepressible handful of people working out of a one-room office in Gainesville, and partly because of the new accent in federal politics on environmental awareness, the river has, at last, been allowed to run in peace.

I wanted to see the "darkly mysterious" Oklawaha with my own eyes. But, on the morning Ben Sanders of the Forest Service had agreed to take me down it in a boat, he came and told me he couldn't make it, because he had to bust some squatters in the Ocala Forest. He said there was a bend in the river, though, which I could get to by walking across a pasture, so I did. A small herd of Jersey cows followed me down to the bank, waded in to their shanks, and began to take long, loud draughts of the cool water. There was a sandy shelf, supported by roots, where the river eddied, and a mixed crowd of sunfish and perch waited to see what it brought them. In the Old South these congregations of milling panfish were known as "jubilees." Five feet out the shelf dropped off and you couldn't see the bottom through the green, mineral-charged water. I took my clothes off, washed them, and spread them out on some cypress roots. The sun had them dry in fifteen minutes. Then I walked out on the shelf, and the cows backed up nervously despite my attempts to calm them. I dove in and started swimming across the current. It was so strong I ended up having to crawl out through some elephantine leaves of fireflag, fifteen feet below the point I'd been making for, even though the river here is only fifty across. I sat on the muddy bank and caught my breath. I'd been doing a lot of traveling, and now, for a few moments, my travels had brought me to the "sweetest water-lane in the world," as Sidney Lanier called it, "a lane which is as if God had turned into water and trees, the recollection of some meditative stroll through the lonely seclusions of his own soul." All the hardwoods of the typical hydric or wet hammock crowded the bank: tupelo, water ash, red bay, sweet gum, red maple, water oak, water hickory, bald cypress, loblolly bay, cabbage palm. Orchids and bromeliads were blooming in the crotches of the trees. There was more here than I could make out without somebody's assistance.

With the Oklawaha still on my mind, I picked up Route 19 and headed south. I stopped where the Nine-Mile Creek runs under the highway and continues through the Ocala Forest. An old man and woman were parked there, fishing away the day from the back of a green camper with Iowa plates. "Any luck?" The man shook his head somewhat irritably. He was casting a worm at several bass that hovered over a sandbar, working with their fins to keep in place. He was too impatient, though—if he'd only left the worm there and let the current bring it down to the fish, they might have taken an interest in it. But the man kept reeling it in jerkily, which just sent the fish scooting into the long wavy grass. Then, after the peculiar disturbance was over, they came out and hovered over the bar again.

Watching the creek snake out through the trees I suddenly developed a powerful need: to get off the pavement, to float a canoe down some winding stream, to follow it through hammocks, swamps, and saw-grass prairies out, finally, to the sea. I was sick of cruising highways and seeing nothing but billboards, road kills, and derelict machinery. Somewhere on the peninsula there ought to be a clean, wild river I could drift down. I started heading south on back roads.

The next day I pulled into the gas station/general store/bar that seemed to be about all there was to the little town of Eva, and looked for someone who could tell me the whereabouts of the Withlacoochee River. According to my road map, it was supposed to cross Highway 33 a few miles north of town. My tires crunched over thousands of bottle caps which had been not merely strewn in the dirt around the pumps, but deliberately inserted as if they were cobblestones. Behind the store, in a shed, were many of the empty beer and soda bottles which had contributed to the paving of the

BEAUTY ON THE BEACH IN FLORIDA   537

pump area. The shed was up on blocks, like most old wooden structures in Florida, which are raised at least eighteen inches from the ground to keep them, hopefully, above termites, floods, and decay. An old cracker with a plug of tobacco in his cheek was sitting in the doorway of the shed. Hardly looking up, he dropped a quid into the dust and answered my inquiry: "This is Eva, all right, but they ain't no river here." In the best of times, he explained, the river didn't usually start running under the road till May, when the rains put an end to the dry season. But now the canals had lowered the water table in the whole area, and the "Little Great Water," which is what the Seminoles had meant by calling it Withlacoochee, hadn't been seen in these parts for three years.

Further down, I discovered, the river was in pretty bad shape too. If I had tried to take it down to the sea, I would have found it blocked at Inglis by the Corps of Engineers, who had diverted seventy-five percent of its flow into the completed piece of the Cross-Florida Barge Canal and left the last seven miles of the river bottom covered with thick silt, which the reduced flow couldn't keep in suspension.

Eva is dead in the middle of the Green Swamp, where three big rivers that empty into the Gulf originate: the Withlacoochee, which flows west and then north; the Hillsborough, which flows south and then west; and the Peace, which flows more or less due south. The Oklawaha also rises partly in the Green Swamp. All these rivers, as well as the other big rivers on the Florida peninsula, flow to the coast in ancient marine troughs. For much of their course they run opposite to the flow of the Floridan Aquifer beneath them, even though they are indebted to it for numerous springs. It's a wonder they aren't sucked down into the Aquifer, but their beds are sealed with clay and are below the level to which the ground water would rise if it were released from its artesian confinement. So, according to some thinking, the rivers are actually buoyed up by pressure from the Aquifer.

By the time the Peace River reaches Zolfo Springs, a small town with a sizable Mexican population several hours below Eva, it is about thirty feet wide. Where Route 17 crosses the Peace, I stopped at a bridge and looked into a hammock where the wind stirred in the branches of laurel and water oaks, bitternut and water hickories, and other moss-hung hardwoods, and the quaking of tree frogs competed with the rattle of cicadas. The water, oddly, was running white, almost the color of milk, spilling over a two-foot ledge, which is a remarkably abrupt change of elevation for lower Florida. There was no sign of life except for rank blooms of algae and occasional patches of water hyacinth.

Below the bridge there was a small public park called Pioneer Park where there were caged examples of the wildlife that once abounded in Florida: several deer and alligators, a black bear, a sandhill crane whose wings had been clipped, and a lynx. Several dozen boat-tailed grackles had squeezed through the mesh of the chain-link fence and were keeping the animals company. Further down, along the riverbank, there was a clearing. A sign said: Site of political rallies held during period of 1900–1925. Here was shaped the destiny of Desoto and Hardee Counties. The clearing is now used as a landing by the Wachula Boat Club. About a dozen skiffs were turned up on the bank, and the club had hired an eighty-year-old man named Cronley Hanchy to keep an eye on things. Mr. Hanchy was taking his nooning with his brother, who was visiting from Virginia. They were sitting under the awning of the caretaker's trailer having ham-and-cheese sandwiches and a quart of beer.

Mr. Hanchy didn't recommend canoeing the Peace River. A few months before, he told me, a phosphate mine at Fort Meade had spilled about a billion gallons of waste chemicals into the river from one of its holding ponds, laying "near to two foot of silt" on the bottom and turning the water that chalky color. It would take several years for the river and its fish, whose food was smothered, to recover, and the state was suing the Cities Service Company, which owns the mine, to the tune of twenty million dollars. "If I was you, I'd try the Kissimmee," he said.

Now, the Kissimmee River (pronounced "Ki-*si*-mee") is a vital link in a complicated water system draining the better part of peninsular Florida. To start, not far from Walt Disney World is the Windermere chain of lakes, which give rise to Cypress Creek, which empties into Bay Lake, which flows southward twenty-five miles into Lake Hatchineha, which is connected by another creek to Lake Kissimmee. The Kissimmee River, finally, spills over the south rim of Lake Kissimmee into a forty-five-thousand-acre floodplain, the winter home of legions of ducks and pasturage for the great cattle ranches of central Florida. Not much grows on this desolate prairie but scattered cypress heads, giant thistles with astonishing rosettes radiating from the base of their stalks, and palmetto fans that are chewed down to stubs by the cows in winter when the grass is dead and rank. It is impossible to tell exactly how long the Kissimmee River is, because as it winds through the floodplain it becomes many rivers. Some fifty miles later, though, all the swampy channels and the meandering fingers collect themselves into one stream, which

empties into Lake Okeechobee. And from the south rim of Okeechobee the water moves again in a shallow sheet of water called by the
Seminoles Pahay-o-kee, "the river of grass," sweeping across Palm
Beach, Broward, and Dade counties and filling the Biscayne
Aquifer, which is the water source for the cities of Fort Lauderdale
and Miami. From here it flows through Everglades National Park
into Cape Sable and, at the very last, Florida Bay.

The ditching of the Kissimmee began between 1881 and 1896,
when Hamilton Disston, heir to the Disston Saw Company of Philadelphia, bought up from the state four million acres in Central
Florida for twenty-four cents an acre. As a preliminary step to creating what he envisioned as a new Garden of Eden, Disston cut
through the major oxbows of the Kissimmee River so that it was
possible to navigate by sidewheeler from the town of Kissimmee all
the way down to Fort Myers, at least when there was water. In 1969
the Army Corps of Engineers realized fully Disston's dream by
reaming the Kissimmee with a grotesque machine whose revolving
cutting head chewed up everything in its path, squirted up the
residue on a spoil bank, and left in its wake Canal C–38, a sterile
ditch one hundred ninety feet wide, twenty-seven feet deep, and
fifty-two miles long. The effects of this project on the Kissimmee-
Okeechobee basin continue to be felt: the river's meanders are
stagnant, choked with water hyacinths, and no longer attractive to
wintering waterfowl; on a recent monthly census flight the Florida
Game and Fish Department counted only fourteen thousand ducks,
where as many as one million six hundred thousand had been
counted in earlier years. Further, all the nutrients that had once been
filtered out of the Kissimmee as it snaked through the marsh are now
pouring directly into Lake Okeechobee, coagulating in a delta of

gray ooze. The lake is showing signs of this overenrichment: an explosion of the waterweed *Hydrilla verticillata* and spectacular algal blooms. I guess that when Mr. Cronley Hanchy told me the Kissimmee was still a clean, wild river, he hadn't gotten wind of these developments.

While the stated aim of its Kissimmee River project was flood control, the Corps of Engineers was not unaware that, by draining the prairie, it had, in fact, "reclaimed" the area as well. The cattle barons of central Florida, some of whom have held key positions in the Central and Southern Flood Control District, the outfit that plans these projects, were naturally pleased by this coincidence. Another party to benefit from the construction of Canal C–38 was the Gulf American Corporation, which has three vast holdings in still-remote Florida wetlands: Golden Gate Estates and Remuda Ranch in the Big Cypress Swamp, and River Ranch Shores on the Kissimmee Prairie. "Strategically located in the path of progress," these lands, figure the GAC people, will one day spawn great cities. And if not, at least GAC will have disposed of enough lots at northern sales banquets to make back its original investment.

Twenty-seven miles west of Yeehaw Junction, Lake Kissimmee flows into the former Kissimmee River, now C–38. And down along the western bank of C–38 is the 57,000-acre "boom area" of River Ranch Shores, which is still desolate prairie except for the first installments of the future city: a dude ranch, a model-home village consisting of a few dozen cinderblock ranch houses, and a five-thousand-foot paved and lighted runway.

One evening at dusk I taxied up to the main lodge at the dude ranch. Everything on the ranch grounds looked like some kind of prop: a covered wagon and stagecoach on a close-cropped lawn surrounded by a white-painted post-and-rail fence; a canteen that sold postcards, films, and cowboy clothes; a motel with a stage-set false front; a simulated saloon that offered draft beer and pizza. On poles planted around the grounds the glowing blue rods of a device called Mr. Insectocutor attracted moths, mosquitoes, and midges, and rubbed them out in a great blue sizzle. Heaps of insects, half disintegrated by the electric charge, lay in the grass below the rods. Parked beside my car, hitched onto the backs of ranch wagons, were two flat-bottomed boats with huge outboard motors, swivel chairs for fighting big-mouth bass, and seats in the middle for the guides. In the lodge, ten or twelve prospects were sitting around a two-story stone fireplace relaxing after a day of fishing, horseback riding, trap shooting, and boar hunting, while hostesses dressed in fringed cowgirl outfits went around making sure they were happy. I asked the man at the front desk if he had any literature about the development. "Sho' nuff." He gave me a brochure that told me how River Ranch Shores offered me "the kind of life where you can wake up in the morning to the songs of red-throat warblers instead of a chorus of horns." In the next room, the mournful pedal-steel guitar of the Buckaroos, the resident country and western band, was bluing notes.

Several hundred yards away Canal C–38 flowed placidly, its spoil bank gleaming ghostly white in the moonlight. In Satellite photographs, the bank, formed of the excavated earth, is the only discernible human artifact in central Florida, showing up as a thin slash across the green prairie. Many seashells, the color of bleached bones, were dredged up with the sand: clams, angel wings, scallops, periwinkles, and channeled whelks—relics of a time when Florida was still a shallow sea. Growing now over the mounds of earth and marine debris are pokeweed and popgun elderberry, through whose hollow

Logging in Florida.

stalks resourceful children can propel spitballs at each other. The flat clusters of white flowers, some of which were already turning into black elderberries, were being worked over by swarms of blackbirds and mourning doves. I didn't see any of the enthusiastically promised red-throated warblers, though, because those creatures had been invented by some man in Chicago or New York, who sits in his office painting pastoral word pictures. Across the canal the white, brown, and black pellets of cattle were sitting and chewing placidly on the prairie.

Some time after that I took a trip up the Loxahatchee River. It drains a vast marshy pool east of Lake Okeechobee called the Loxahatchee Slough and flows into Jupiter Inlet on the Atlantic Coast. Reliable sources had assured me that *it* was the last clean, wild river on the peninsula. My guide was Nils Frieburg, a native of Rockaway Beach, New York, who has been conducting jungle cruises up the Loxahatchee for the last fifteen years in an open flatboat. Frieburg is probably as familiar with the river as anyone. While retaining a distinct Brooklyn accent, he has become, in the opinion of some, the most accomplished alligator caller in the state of Florida, outside of maybe Ross Allen, the director of the Ross Allen Reptile Institute at Silver Springs. One misty morning, killing the engine of his flatboat several hundred yards above a landing in Jonathan Dickinson State Park, Frieburg began to produce a strange mixture of grunts and quacks from deep in his throat. At first nothing happened. Frieburg continued making noises for the better part of a minute, until at last something big stirred in a thicket of pond apples and cocoa plums decked with poison ivy and defoliated by tent caterpillars. "Come on, George, come out here," Frieburg said, and an eight-foot log with black, deeply furrowed bark eased into the river and drifted quietly toward us. Frieburg unwrapped a packet of cheese crackers with peanut-butter filling and tossed one at the advancing reptile, who raised the broad, blunt snout that distinguishes alligators from crocs and chomped down on it. In two years, he told me, George and the other alligators who drifted up to his boat, faithfully snapped up crackers and marshmallows, and struck the fear of God into his passengers would be driven out by salt-water intrusion. A wealthy West Palm Beach contractor, John D. Macarthur, had dug a canal deep in the Loxahatchee Slough to drain off an area he was fixing to develop. When asked about the canal, Macarthur had reportedly looked surprised and said, "What canal?" It had lowered the river five feet and salted it for about twelve miles, up to its first weir.

"Two years from now, this will all be gone," Frieburg told me, indicating the whole strand of virgin royal palms and bald cypresses. He showed me a huge cypress, a good twenty feet around and sixty high, which he said had stood there for at least five hundred years and was now about to topple, dangling by one last thread of root, the rest of its base eroded by the salting of the river in the last year. Twenty feet up a pileated woodpecker was boring into the tree, its staccato jabs echoing up and down the waterway. Frieburg pulled up to the bank and had me taste some cocoa plums. It was too soon for pond apples, he said. In two years he predicted the only trees here would be salt-loving red mangroves.

In the last ten thousand years, because of shrinking polar icecaps and shifts in the earth's crust, the sea has been gradually encroaching on the land. One calculation has the sea rising about two and a half inches every hundred years.

In Florida, the salt-water encroachment is being speeded up by the digging of canals and the pumping-out of fresh water. Under normal conditions the sea is kept from creeping into the peninsula's porous limestone by a dynamic balance between the ground water and the sea. To equalize the pressure of the heavier salt water, the fresh-water head has to be at least two feet higher than the mean sea level in most places, or else the salt water will move in laterally and from beneath. Much of the encroachment comes during droughts when the sea creeps up the mouths of drainage canals and rivers like the Loxahatchee. In 1925 Miami's wells, one and a half miles inland, were contaminated, and so were moved inland five more miles. By 1939, the sea had reached the new wells. In 1930, because of salt-water intrusion, St. Petersburg abandoned its local wells and sought a new water supply thirty-seven miles inland in northwest Hillsborough County. Since the thirties, Tampa has had to get its water from the Hillsborough River, because the local ground water is periodically impregnated by the sea. Salt-water intrusion is a problem throughout southern Florida, and it is getting worse.

The more rivers I visited, the more I got the feeling that I had come too late, and that even what was left of them wasn't going to be around much longer. One Saturday two Gainesville boys and their girl friends took me down to the Crystal River, a short one on the Gulf side which is almost entirely fed by springs. We put in a canoe and a small outboard and went to see the manatees, or sea cows, who make their winter hibernaculum in the boil of a spring that stays seventy-two degrees year round. While tree swallows with glistening blue backs skimmed the water and a large, silent flotilla of coots glided by, we dove into the river and swam with the blimp-like manatees, who are relatives of the elephant. The giant mammals weigh up to a ton and have virtually no features except for their cowlike snouts and tiny eyes. They chased each other around at surprising speeds with effortless flicks of their tails, and although we couldn't keep up with them, we could see them easily through the cloudy water and the flashing swarms of mullet because of white propeller scars on their backs. Manatees eat up to a hundred pounds of aquatic plants a day, including the waterweed *Hydrilla verticillata,* which infests the Crystal and other coastal rivers. The gentle creatures, who seem to lack all fear of man, have lent their name to a county, a medical center, and dozens of namable entities in Florida. But every year dozens of manatees, gentle or not, are killed by motorboats barrelassing up the channels that they've cleared and by young pranksters who drop rocks on them from bridges. Only a few hundred are left in Florida.

Hydrilla verticillata, on the other hand, is all over the place, its long, wavering strands, with small, narrow leaves attached to the stems in clusters of three that bunch up at the tip, rooted to the bottom of lakes, rivers, and canals. Imported from Southeast Asia as an aquarium plant, hydrilla escaped into ponds and streams near Tampa in 1946 and is now believed to infest thirty-five thousand acres of fresh-water bottom. One of the fastest-growing, fastest-reproducing underwater flowering plants in the world, it grows two inches a day, gets to be twenty feet long, and has no natural enemy in Florida other than the manatee. Broken shoots of the plant drift downstream, attach themselves to the bottom by fine roots, and develop into new plants. Rooted hydrilla sends out underground shoots with swollen tips that sprout into new stems. Sprigs of hydrilla are taken around the peninsula on boat propellers and in the feet of birds. Animals eat the fruit of their tiny flowers and drop the seeds in new locations. If you kill the plant with copper sulfate it covers the bottom with a rotting mat that smothers everything except for lower organisms like worms and leeches. Attempts to remove it mechanically have proved difficult and costly, and anyhow, it grows right back. In one experiment made several years ago, a school of the Nile perch Tilapia was brought in from Egypt and released in a pond to see how it would do with the hydrilla. The fish is supposed to be herbivorous, but it turned out that the wrong species of Tilapia —a voracious breeder that wouldn't take a hook and outcompeted the native species—had been imported. Well, the perch cleaned out the hydrilla, the native fish, and everything else and then fertilized the water with excrement until it became soupy and overenriched instead of clear and weed-infested—and that was an open invitation for water hyacinths. Then people came and netted the perch and let them go in neighboring lakes. Today Lake Griffin is estimated to have thirty-five hundred pounds of Tilapia per acre, while the average density of the native species there had been three to five hundred pounds per acre.

As I continued my quest for a river that was clean and wild, I was slowly forced to the dismal conclusion that there were none, at least not on the peninsula. All of them have been done in in one way or another. Even the obscure Fisheating Creek, which feeds Lake Okeechobee, has become a victim of drainage canals. Even the Myakka River, whose dark waters travel to the Gulf through remote palm-flecked savannas, is in bad shape. At the Snookhaven Fish Camp, on an oxbow of the Myakka, a man with a shirt that said MARTIN CONCRETE on its back, playing pool with a woman whose left arm had the initials JR tattooed on it, explained that the river rises in cattle country and is heavily polluted for several days when it rains.

A Swami Convention

Back in the early sixties there was plenty of room in Orlando, and so the planning folks who designated Route 50 west of Kirkland Avenue as their local "miracle mile" were able to accomplish big things. They put in the highway six lanes wide and gave it a center strip, and they acquired the nearby truck farms and gladiola fields so that they could install the great shopping plazas and car sales lots and the featureless seas of blacktop. Today this stretch of Route 50 is known as West Colonial Drive, and it is probably the most monumental strip in Florida, rolling across the old sea floor so flat and wide and low in the sky you can see it coming for miles. It begins with a Lincoln-Mercury dealer, and for the next three miles just about every business enterprise that has anything to do with your automobile, and many other business enterprises as well, can be found there.

The most conspicuous ornament of West Colonial Drive is a twenty-foot torso of a man with black glasses, silver sideburns, and a green plaid sports coat, mounted on a gigantic white plastic cube, in front of Art Grindle's Dodge dealership on the corner of Pine Hill Road. This remarkable figure is, in fact, an enlargement in fiberglass of none other than Art Grindle himself. Its right arm rises and falls stiffly at the elbow, forefinger pointing, as if it were trying to tell you something. Since Art Grindle's company motto is "I want to sell you a car," this is most likely what the statue is trying to tell you. It is a well-known landmark around Orlando, and you really don't even have to go to West Colonial Drive to see it, because it is shown in commercials during the weekend theatres on Channels 2, 6, and 9.

Art Grindle himself, a recent arrival from Chicago, is an outstanding example of the northern brains and energy that have helped make Florida what it is today. An ordinary-looking guy with black glasses, silver sideburns, and, in real life, a sharply cut continental suit rather than the plaid sportscoat of the statue, he was, when I found him, sitting in his office at the beginning of a long row of consultation chambers, smoking and going over sales charts with a subordinate. He looked up for a moment as my shadow fell across his desk, sized me up, and asked me what I wanted. When I said I just wanted to chat for a bit he winced visibly, his worst fears—that I had *not* come to buy—confirmed, and told me to come back the next day.

In a few short years Grindle has become the head of a big, fast operation. There are two men waiting full time in the parking lot just to welcome the customers as they step out of their cars, and to escort them to the showroom. One of these is a tall young black who goes by the name of Fast Frank, wears high-heeled shoes, satin shirts, and has a big-toothed comb sunk into his hair. Inside the showroom the latest Dodges turn slowly around, and a huge sailfish hangs on the wall. A salesman stands at parade rest in front of the picture window, waiting to lead the customers into the consultation chambers, to sit them down in black leather easy chairs, and to sell them the car suited to their individual life style.

Across the street the lot is empty, and a riot of weeds is enjoying a transient existence there, until some businessman comes along who has what it takes to rival Grindle and his great fiberglass alter ego. There are enough plants "whose virtue," as Emerson wrote, "has not yet been discovered," to make your head swim. Some are natives, others came from other continents in the holds of ships and on the clothing of immigrants. Included are the likes of ragweed, horseweed, bitter sneezeweed, bull thistle, dog fennel, galinsoga, mustard, castor bean, dandelion, and daisy. In the midst of this vagrant vegetable confusion an egret stands calmly on a Lamar billboard that announces a Holiday Inn's "Fine Food and Lodging Two Miles Ahead." Another billboard in the lot says, YOU GOTTA LOVE THE GUYS. ORANGE BUICK-OPEL LOVES PEOPLE. Behind the signs is a little cypress island whose branches are matted with Spanish moss.

If Grindle's operation is an example of the Yankee way of doing business, Pete Murray, whose modest fleet of used cars resides under a canopy of idly fluttering streamers and pennants half a mile further down West Colonial Drive, typifies the laissez-faire southern approach to selling cars. In 1883 a northern journalist named George M. Barbour wrote of the native crackers of Florida that they were "a block in the pathway of civilization, settlement, and enterprise wherever they exist." Well, Pete Murray is a cracker and proud of it. He exists, surrounded by his cars, in a one-room shack that says

"Streamlining through Wonderful Florida"

NOTARY PUBLIC on the door. I found him there later that afternoon taking a nap in a red reclining chair before a white gas heater. An old white poodle was doing the same on the floor beside him. Murray is sixty-two, a native of Tampa, has been in Florida "all ma laf," and on "the boulevard," as he calls it, for the past ten years. "I sold the first car I ever sold in 1925," he recalls. "Hit was a Star." In back of him a calendar that has a picture of a Model T Ford shows the dates for December, 1917, which all fall on the same days of the week as those in December, 1973. Murray buys his cars "right off the curb" and pays spot cash for them. Everything in his lot sells for under two hundred dollars—old crates that people might want for second or third cars or to get them to work and back—"just pure ol' scrap iron," he admits, "but it's a way for 'em to go. An' it beats walkin'."

Murray has one assistant, an old cuss who chews tobacco, talks with the people who drive up, and only goes and fetches Murray if it looks like a deal is in the making. Murray doesn't like to get up any more than he has to, since he has a wooden leg and has to use a crutch. Outside the window his assistant is talking with a man who looks Cuban or Puerto Rican. "We sell a lot of our cars to these heah transient farm labor who work in the orange groves and gladiola fields," Murray says. Most of his business as a notary public is title work, signing the cars over from one owner to another. "You know," he says, complaining a little, "hit takes a fairly crime-free background to get a license as a car dealer. Even then most people think we're crooks."

Across the boulevard is the state prison farm. Three inmates in blue fatigues are leaning on a railing on a ramp below the sooty stacks of the farm's incinerator, surveying the action on West

Colonial Drive. This side of the fence a billboard invites everybody to drop in at the First Baptist Church of Pine Hills. The bland face of the bespectacled Reverend Bill Sutton asks the question, "What's missing?" Missing from the middle of the word church are the letters "UR."

My old car and I pulled up at the corner of West Colonial Drive and Pine Hill Road and waited docilely for a green light. With me were a seventeen-year-old longhair who had recently changed his name from Randy to Thousand-Petal Lotus, and two sixteen-year-old hippie girls, Patti and Karen. It was after dark. The businesses on the strip had turned their signs on. The top of my convertible was down, leaving us exposed to the elements, especially neon. Overhead, the forearm of Art Grindle's giant rose and fell, pointing significantly.

Thousand-Petal Lotus and the two hippie girls are followers of an Indian holy man named Yogi Bajan, who had arrived in Los Angeles at a time when there was great spiritual hunger in America. Bajan promptly founded the Happy, Healthy, Holy Organization, and developed a following of young people who were disillusioned with marijuana and psychedelic drugs, but were still seeking an alternative to what Randy a.k.a. Thousand-Petal Lotus calls "nouveau-grosso plasticana." Now the 3 H-O has a hundred ashrams, or spiritual retreats, around the country, and the Baba Sirchand Ashram in Orlando had been chosen as the one where the followers would convene with their guru for a ten-day celebration of the winter solstice.

The ashram is in a pine woods smack in the middle of a strait-laced suburb of cinderblock ranchhouses. Across the street, for example, on a cul-de-sac called Pipes of the Glen Road, live a state cop, an electrician who works at nearby Disney World, and a retired rubber worker from Akron, Ohio. The Christian religion is still going strong here, judging from the number of churches in the neighborhood. So, naturally, when two hundred young folks wearing turbans and coming from as far away as Manitoba arrived one day in dilapidated vans, retired schoolbuses, psychedelic panel trucks, and other rigs, and proceeded to camp in the woods of the ashram, they caused quite a sensation. At first the town commissioners, who were deluged with phone calls, said there wasn't any place within a hundred miles that was zoned for a "swami convention," but finally one of them allowed as how it would be okay if the swami and his followers camped in the back corner of the Green Acres Trailer Park, a few miles away, as long as they didn't make any trouble. Now, the Green Acres Trailer Park might strike some people as a peculiar place for a swami convention. Half the people in it are wintering retirees who stay for three to five months; the rest are vacationers who come from all over creation to see Disney World. And, sure enough, nobody there knew quite what to make of a strange turbaned element that suddenly took over the back of the park, sat cross-legged in circles and chanted in a foreign tongue every morning till the sun went up. The rumor was they were reformed heroin addicts. But Yogi Bajan had ordered his followers to "cool it." They did so, and kept to themselves, and the Green Acres people left it at that.

The light changed, and we moved on through the neon nighttime on West Colonial Drive. After a week of nothing but rice, bananas, potatoes, and assorted greens, Patti, Karen, and Thousand-Petal Lotus had a hankering for some good solid, all-American pizza.

Thousand-Petal Lotus took off his turban, which he said had taken him roughly forty-five minutes that morning to wind around his head. Underneath it his hair was tied in a rishi knot, which is supposed to trap the solar energy that falls down on his head, while the turban is needed to ward off harmful electromagnetic waves. Thousand-Petal Lotus said he'd been learning all these breathing exercises that were designed to bring up the *kundalini,* or creative energy of the universe, from the base of his spine. These exercises had been getting him "naturally stoned" and higher than he'd ever been on psychedelic drugs. In fact he and Patti and Karen were so high that they were constantly hugging each other and laughing. When we finally gave up our search for pizza and settled for a Howdyburger place, an indefinable aura of health, happiness, and holiness seemed to hover around our booth. The young waitress who took our order noticed it, and even started glowing and giggling a bit herself. This, Thousand-Petal explained to me, is known as a "contact high."

The Green Acres Trailer Park is one of the largest facilities "For the Pampered Camper" in the entire state of Florida. The size of three football fields put together, it is advertised by seventy-eight billboards and a hundred thousand brochures distributed around the state and has seven hundred and forty-eight grass-carpeted sites with hookups for gas and electric, five bathhouses, a coin laundry, a recreation hall with color TV's and pinball machines, and a canteen that sells beer, propane, postcards, Green Acres Trailer Park sweatshirts, and other vital equipment. It is within easy reach of Route 4, Highway 441, and the Bee-line Thruway, yet nestled among orange groves that muffle the noise of traffic. To get to it you take a left at a drive-in where the likes of *Big Sur, Bangladesh,* and *Vanishing Point* are triple-featured, then continue into a predominantly black sub-

division, which flanks the park on two sides. The park is surrounded on all sides by an eight-foot chain-link fence. About fifty yards beyond the back corner of Green Acres, where the followers of Yogi Bajan were camped, there is a small white building with a steeple called the New Providence Baptist Church.

Now the swami convention ended on a Sunday morning with a mass wedding in which the guru married ten couples and pronounced the engagement of eight more. One of the couples decided to get married right on the spot, at Bajan's suggestion. "See how you vibe on each other," he had told them, and apparently they had liked each other well enough to go ahead with it. "These flash weddings work pretty well," Thousand-Petal Lotus told me. "There's no time for romance. The body isn't important. It's spirit that counts, and everybody's got that."

The back corner of the Green Acres Trailer Park was resplendent with white turbans, shawls, saris, Nehru jackets, and the bright raiment of relatives who had flown down for the ceremony and were sitting in deck chairs. Even the little man on the many-tiered wedding cake had on a turban. Two little black boys and an immature white-throated sparrow were clinging to the chain-link fence, taking in the ceremony. After some delay Yogi Bajan arrived in a sedan with a small entourage which escorted him to a sort of niche that had been prepared for him, where he assumed the lotus position on a pillow under a canopy of printed Indian cloth.

The guru was a large, earthy man in his fifties, dressed entirely in white. He seemed to be in pain, as if suffering from indigestion, and on the surface he seemed to be no more holy than you or I. He began to lecture the couples in a high, mellifluous voice on the gravity of what they were getting into, going on about how marriage in America is a sexual convenience, while it is really an eternal union between two souls, for which the participants should maintain an "attitude of gratitude" for the rest of their lives. Then he held up his hands and said, "In your lives, dear children . . ." and I couldn't catch the rest because at that moment the congregation of the New Providence Baptist Church broke out singing, "God told Nicodemus, You must be born again," punctuating it with the shaking and slapping of tambourines, the clapping of hands, the sobbing of sin-sick souls, and the boisterous shouting of "Amen" and "Praise the Lord." In the middle of the singing two deacons of the church carried out a three-hundred-pound woman in a green choir robe who had apparently just been born again. Her face was beaded with sweat and her eyelids were a-flutter. They left her out on the steps with several women, who revived her with fans donated by a local funeral home. The ground in front of her had been beaten hard by the feet of running children. Three children were playing a game that involved hitting a tin can with a broomstick and running around two black Cadillacs. A few minutes later, in the final moments of Bajan's ceremony, the congregation of the New Providence Baptist Church came out into the sunshine, led by their bow-tied minister, the Reverend Allen Majors of the Bahamas, whose glowing countenance contrasted sharply with the dyspeptic looking Indian guru on the other side of the fence. Asked what he thought of the Happy, Healthy, Holy Organization, the preacher shook his head and said, "I dunno," then, beaming brightly, "Well, I guess there's hypocrites in every group."

The Magic Kingdom

That morning, I fell in with a procession of campers that trickled out of the Green Acres Trailer Park in Orlando, making its way toward Disney World. At the same time, in fact, all over central Florida other cars with the same destination were debouching from trailer parks, campgrounds, and motels, and before long all of us converged on Route 4. By eleven o'clock we were backed up solid for eighteen miles and a sober-visaged newsman was standing in the emergency lane explaining the situation to a TV camera. Only once before, an old-timer told me later, had Florida been so inundated with traffic, when hundreds of thousands came in flivvers to make their fortune in the '24 land boom. Today there were more cars than the six lanes leading to Disney World could possibly accommodate, and by two o'clock its seventy-thousand-car parking lot was filled, and signs went up on Route 4 telling the thousands of people who had been waiting there for hours to turn around and try again tomorrow. I was one of the last cars to make it into the Magic Kingdom that day.

Beaming blond boys in orange uniforms flagged me around different sections of the parking lot, which were named after the Seven Dwarfs. At last I taxied to rest beside a late-model Chevrolet that was just disgorging a family from Kentucky. The son was a lance corporal in the Marines, dressed in his full winter service Alpha uniform. I knew from experience how hot and disagreeable that heavy green wool was, but the brave lad was showing no signs of discomfort. We all piled into a tram, and as we pulled out the driver reminded us that we had parked in "Bashful."

An hour later, having waited on line, I had secured my ticket book and was standing at one end of Main Street, wondering whether to take a horse-drawn trolley, a fire truck, or an old-fashioned double-decker bus to the castle at the other end, whereupon I would have to choose again, this time among the pleasures of Adventureland, Frontierland, Fantasyland, Tomorrowland, and Liberty Square. Thousands of people were milling around me, licking cones and staring into boutique windows. Right in with them, the likes of Mickey Mouse, Goofy, Snow White, the Seven Dwarfs, and others were milling too, nodding benignly, shaking hands, signing autographs, posing for pictures, and letting the children see that they were real. High above, through a hidden speaker, Tinkerbell was singing: "A dream is a wish your heart makes when you're fast asleep." Suddenly the song stopped and a voice came on instructing everybody to clear the road. We all stood on the curb and broke into involuntary goose bumps as the strump of drums drew near. It was a parade led by the Disney characters, who had ducked out of the crowd. They were followed by a band that marched with the stiff precision of wooden soldiers. None of the men behind the instruments, I observed, had pot bellies or sloppy posture. They had accuracy but no soul, not like that displayed by the color guard of the all-black New Rochelle post of the American Legion as they march through Bedford, New York, in the Firemen's Carnival Parade, throwing their dummy rifles back and forth. No one was looped, like the old cuss who rides a hay wagon through the town of Warner, New Hampshire, during the Fall Foliage Festival, waving a jug of hard cider. No girls blushed or dropped their batons, as I've seen the Immaculate Conception Rockettes do marching through Concord, Massachusetts, on the anniversary of the shot heard round the world, their gray flannel skirts down to their ankles and a nun on either side of them. Not a flat note was blown by the tubas, not a clarinet squeaked. Thousands of balloons were released as the band passed. An hour later they came out and did it all over again.

I waited in a penny arcade for a chance to see *Steamboat Willie,* Walt Disney's first animated cartoon. Mickey Mouse *ca.* 1928 was a scrawny, four-fingered stick figure whose comic repertoire was limited to playing vibes on the teeth of a milk cow, cracking corny barnyard jokes, and foiling the attempts of Captain Cat to navigate a sidewheeler to Podunk Landing. When I returned to the present, dozens of beaming blond boys in orange uniforms were skewering litter on pointed sticks. Beneath me, some of the fifty tons of refuse that forty thousand visitors generate daily were being whisked through vacuum tubes at sixty miles per hour from fifteen stations to the central compacting plant of the complex's Swedish AVAC garbage system. I joined hundreds of fellow Americans who were being marshaled by girls in riding clothes, armed with crops which they used as pointers. Forty-five minutes later I stepped into a boat with a family from Milwaukee. "Sure feels good to sit down again," the father sighed to me. Beaming blond attendants lifted his ten-year-old daughter, whose shriveled legs were in braces, from a wheelchair and lowered her into the boat. The child's eyes widened as the gently flowing water took us past groups of dolls from foreign lands singing in different tongues, past smiling green kangaroos with babies, elephants with tummy aches, glittering butterflies, birds hatching repeatedly from the same egg, little Cossack dancers, assorted angels, Arabian knights, hula girls, spinning ferris wheels, and swaying flowers singing a catchy tune called "It's a Small, Small World."

After an even longer wait with a troop of Boy Scouts from Bayonne, New Jersey (there was a slight delay while attendants hunted for a contact lens lost in the last show), I was admitted to the Country Bear Jamboree. The entire show was given by an ensemble of "audio-animatronic" bears, great big rubber dolls with supple, computer-driven lips who sat down and got up and talked to each other and did just about everything short of taking steps. One of them, with a pink ballet skirt on, went by the name of Liver-Lips McGraw. When she puckered up and sang in a husky voice, "All the guys that turn me on turn me down," the heart-rending lyric elicited five minutes of whistling and stomping from Bayonne's Troop 401. As the show ended a bear named Big Al thanked everybody for "bearing with us to the bear end." The chief executives in the Hall of Presidents were also audio-animatronic dummies. All of them got up and said things except for FDR, who remained seated. They were far more animated than their audience, which stood there quietly, deeply moved, as they watched a film that summarized U.S. history in twelve minutes. No one was allowed to take pictures.

There were plastic hippopotami that yawned at me on the jungle cruise, mermaids who wriggled by the portholes of Captain Nemo's

On an Alligator Farm, Florida

Nautilus, and the Monsanto exhibit, where a thousand of us at a time were enveloped by nine synchronized screens that took us on a trip from New York City to California. It was so terribly real that we hugged each other for dear life, as our cars, planes, and fire engines grazed the roofs of a Vermont covered bridge and practically collided with the walls of the Grand Canyon.

By this time, it was getting dark. I had spent eight hours in Disney World, a good deal of it in line, and I didn't know if I was coming or going. A recording of crickets started up in a plastic jungle below the Swiss Family Robinson's house in a cement tree. I flipped a dime over a bridge into a canal that glistened with coins and wished the children of Florida good luck in the years to come. Then I threw in another dime and wished them luck again, and followed it with a quarter and some pennies, which exhausted my change. I gave my ticket book with its two remaining events to Waldemar Kissel, a ten-year-old boy from Cologne, Germany, sitting in the Sleepy Hollow Restaurant with his grandmother taking a breather. Leaving the restaurant, I started to run. Through the gates of the Magic Kingdom to where people were waiting for trams to return them to their cars, past beaming blond attendants in orange uniforms, into a garden inhabited only by Disney characters cut out of green plastic shrubs. I slowed down as there loomed ahead of me a huge concrete building shaped like the letter A. Inside, a four-story plastic Christmas tree flickered blindingly, and a choir of flaxen-haired Florida boys and girls with warmup jackets, bobby socks, saddle shoes, and long scarves strolled around arm in arm singing " 'Tis the Season to Be Jolly." A bullet-shaped car pulled up on a monorail and discharged passengers, who trundled off to the more than one thousand rooms that overlook the Grand Canyon Concourse. A plainclothesman accosted three suspicious longhairs and asked them to go along with him. They just snickered, until he said something into a walkie-talkie, whereupon they went along quite meekly.

Finally I found my way back to Bashful and spotted my Dynamic 88 immediately, sticking out like a pair of wornout sneakers in a sea of spitshined loafers. Out there in the parking lot, getting ready to get into my car, I exchanged a few words with some people called Ken and Grace Prindle as they were getting into theirs. They had been at Disney World since eight that morning, having spent the night at the Blue Parrot Campground one hour north. Ken Prindle is hulking, jovial, fifty-seven; a true Connecticut Yankee, who says "round" instead of "rung" when speaking of ladders; calls a gutter an "eavestrough," an earthworm an "angleworm," Virginia creeper "English ivy," and pronounces "root" to rhyme with "soot." An easygoing but eminently practical man who can make do with what-ever's at hand, he is the "super" for a five-hundred-acre spread in Greenwich, Connecticut. His wife cleans houses in the neighbor-hood. Both are unordained "born again" Baptist ministers. A sticker that said HONK IF YOU KNOW JESUS was affixed to the rear bumper of their car. They had enjoyed Disney World, but felt that, as Grace put it, it was basically "just one big whirl of nothing." "I'm glad I saw it, but I sure wouldn't come all the way to Florida to see it again."

"Oh, it's something all right," Ken conceded. "But I don't go for all that new amusement really." He confided that, anyway, the fact of the matter is that he is partly color-blind. He can see a deer moving through the woods, but he can't pick out strawberries in a field. "So I suppose I couldn't make out a good deal of Disney World anyway," he said, chuckling softly. With that he doffed his polka-dot pork-pie hat, and Ken and Grace Prindle got into their car. I stood there watching as they pulled out of their spot and accelerated into the sunset.

Richard and the Wood Storks

I found Ken Alvarez on a path in Highlands Hammock State Park, planting a label in front of a wild sour-orange tree. This was the part of his job as state naturalist he refers to as "show biz." Alvarez is thirty-four, a big man in his prime who gets extremely restless if he has to be indoors for any length of time. Descended from early Spanish settlers, he grew up on his grandparents' farm near Ocala, and except for a four-year hitch in the Marines which took him to Cuba, Puerto Rico, and Europe, he has never been out of state. In his spare time he goes canoeing, and now that he has the thirteen state parks of southwest Florida to keep track of, he gets to spend more time on the water than ever. "When they handed me my first assignment," he recalled, "which was to canoe a hundred-mile river, I just about dropped."

Florida has seventy-three state parks, seventy-three scraps of untouched wilderness where a visitor can stop and pull things into perspective. Highlands Hammock is in the heart of the state, at the latitude (about twenty-eight degrees north) where cabbage palms begin to figure prominently in the landscape. The nearest outpost of civilization is Sebring, a small railroad town which comes alive each year to host the week-long International Grand Prix auto races. The hammock itself is a young stand of live oaks and cabbage palms which are choking out the last half-dead pines of a flatwoods that used to occupy the site. Along the park's western edge, Little Charley Bowlegs Creek runs into a cypress stand, creating the first southern swamp I ever set foot upon.

"This here's the U.S. Champion cabbage palm, for what that's worth," Alvarez said, pointing to a thin, undulating palm which for some reason had shot up above the other trees to the championship height of ninety feet. A catwalk led us on out over the still, black water of the swamp, where an egret was wading stealthily among buttressed trunks of bald cypress. High above an open pool where the creek ventured out of the trees, fifty or so black and turkey vultures were riding thermals, their shadows moving ominously over the vegetation. An orb-weaver spider had spun a web clear across the pool and was waiting for something to blunder into it. We heard two otters having a row over something, chasing each other all over the swamp. Suddenly a flock of white ibises coasted in through the trees, landed, and promptly began to jab the water with long pink bills. Their luminous pallor was intense as they fed silently in the deep shadows, occasionally squealing or honking as they shook down a wriggling killifish and readjusted their black-tipped wings. A red-shouldered hawk, apparently intrigued by their success, landed in the middle of them, and they took off together, leaving the hawk alone on a cypress knee.

Alvarez wasn't sure why the submerged roots of the cypresses

T.S. 4.—Six Varieties of Sponges, from Left:
Wire, Wool, Silk, Finger, Grass (Vase), Yellow

surface every once in a while to form these "knees." They may be extra support for the trees in their unstable bedding of muck, or what are called "pneumatophores," which conduct air to the sunken roots. When the parent tree is cut, the knees die, but you can lop off a knee, and nothing will happen to the tree. When they are injured by fire, deer, or falling limbs, or by wildcats, who like to sharpen their claws on them, the knees take on strange shapes as the bark heals over.

Coming out in the hammock again, we saw a mangy-looking yellow-bellied sapsucker drilling even rows of holes as it backed down the branch of a big live oak. We drove into Sebring for a dinner of catfish and hush puppies. Later, we returned and felt our way back along the catwalk through pitch blackness. "Come on, I want to show you something," Alvarez said. Searching the darkness with a flashlight, he shined up the eyes of the swamp creatures. There were savage white gleams on the trunks of the cypresses (fisher spiders), a pair of blood-red eyes lurking in the water (alligator), a small pair of red ones above a branch (barred owl), some pink ones (spadefoot toad), and orange ones (most likely a raccoon).

In the morning we got up early and went birding. Our field glasses kept clouding over from the mist, but we were rewarded with the sight of a pileated woodpecker. I overheard a Carolina wren whistling to himself in a bayhead and took in many other noises I'd never heard before. Walking along next to a barbed-wire fence we saw a loggerhead shrike impaling a frog on one of the tines for future consumption. Some birds, like the shrike, which has found barbed wire suited to its sinister purposes, can take human changes to the landscape in their stride. The phoebe that nested in my outhouse in New Hampshire, using as her platform a stack of bills and alumni bulletins I had jammed into a crack in the wall, had no trouble at all.

That morning, an hour after I left Alvarez, I passed a wood stork feeding in a flooded ditch. This fascinating creature, the only stork in North America, has many other names—wood ibis, gourdhead, flinthead, ironhead, preacher, Spanish buzzard—and it is, unfortunately, one of the animals that has not been able to adjust to what man is doing to South Florida.

It was a strange bird that waded in this ditch, with its bald, scaly black knob of a head and a stout bill groping in the muddy water, feeding not by sight but by "tactolocation." Whenever something grazed its mandibles, they would open and snap shut in about twenty milliseconds, and in this way it gnashed up its daily quota of aquatic life. In the air, wood storks are the picture of grace, their great white wings spread motionless to reveal black inner margins; they are the largest of the white wading birds. I saw some a few days later from a canoe on Homestead Canal in the Everglades, spiraling in the thermals of daybreak, performing what Audubon described as "the most beautiful evolutions that can be well conceived." There are some stork rookeries in the Everglades, but most of the birds nest in the crowns of the pre-Columbian cypresses in Corkscrew Swamp. Alvarez said they ought to be on their nests in Corkscrew by now. "Be sure and go there, if it's the only thing you see in Florida."

I got to Corkscrew just at dusk on New Year's Eve. Situated in a remote part of Collier County and under water half the year, it had been inaccessible until 1954, when the National Audubon Society acquired it as a sanctuary. The Audubon people built a boardwalk that penetrated the swamp over a mile, stopping finally at the edge of an interior marsh that is going dry. Coastal-plain willows are coming into the saw grass of this eight-hundred acre clearing, which is secluded on all sides by virgin cypresses, some of them seven hundred years old and a hundred thirty feet high. As a throwback to the cold winters in which they had evolved, the cypresses stood leafless, though there was no need here for them to do so. In the tops of the outermost trees there were big wicker nests, but no storks. The birds were scattered all over Florida, wating for auspicious conditions before they would mass for the flight to their rookery. I had seen hundreds of them on Sanibel Island a few days before, standing beside a water hazard on a golf course.

Almost immediately I ran into Gerry Cutlip, the resident natural-ist, patrolling the boardwalk on a bicycle. He explained that storks breed from January to April, earlier than most birds, because during these months their diet of sunfish, golden shiners, and gambusia is concentrated in drying pools and ditches, giving them the extra fuel they need to undertake the rigors of nesting. But if there has been a drought the summer before, and the fish haven't reproduced in sufficient numbers, the storks won't even try to nest. Droughts have been more frequent since 1959, when the Gulf American Corpora-tion dug a large canal several miles away to prepare for the future city of North Golden Gate. Since that time the hydroperiod in the swamp hasn't been the same. By January the swamp dries up to what used to be the April level, when the water was lowest. "Every time you dig one of these canals, it's like pulling the plug out of a bath-tub," Cutlip commented. Since the canal was excavated, he added, the storks have missed three nesting seasons. The previous year, six hundred storks had produced about as many fledglings, but they had had to fly clear to Lake Okeechobee to get their food—a round trip of sixty miles every day. This year there were only five inches of water in the swamp, and Cutlip said there had to be eleven before

Wood Ibis and
Whooping Crane,
Florida.

the storks would come, judging from their behavior other years. Two weeks later there was a heavy rain, and the storks flew into Corkscrew and took up residence. The year after that there was plenty of rain, but no food in the water, and the birds didn't nest anywhere in Florida.

It was during the days of waiting for the storks to arrive that a naturalist couldn't help having black thoughts. All it would take was for the birds to miss several nesting seasons in a row, and they could pass out of this world entirely. In 1954, Alexander Sprunt, Jr., wrote in his *Florida Bird Life* that the wood stork "enjoys a rather static condition of well-being in Florida." But that has changed. A report written in 1969 arguing against the construction of a jetport in the adjacent Big Cypress Swamp described the current chances of this magnificent, highly specialized creature:

> The U.S. stands to lose at least 50% of its wood ibis population if the critical feeding grounds in the Big Cypress are drained. In this species and other wading birds that nest in dense colonies, social stimulation plays a major role in nesting success. Below some lower limit of colony size, nesting often fails regardless of ecological conditions. This exact point of no return is not known.

I left the willow-infested marsh and returned to my convertible. The nearest town was Immokalee, a migrant-labor center, where I figured I'd celebrate New Year's with a shower. I started down the road with the top down, scaring up turkey buzzards: they had it down to a science, timing themselves to rise from their dinner of flattened rabbits at the last possible second. A loose pack of egrets floated in the distance like snowflakes, and all the way to Immokalee

I followed the end of a thick rainbow that disappeared into the steel-gray sky. Halfway there I picked up a flock of seven wood storks following the road, averaging about twenty-five miles an hour, flapping and sailing in spurts, their legs joined straight out behind them, bobbing slightly as they picked up the beat again. They left me at the edge of town.

I took Room 36 in a fruit-pickers' flophouse—$3.12 for the night. No lock. After checking it out, I went to the lobby, where the Coke machine took my money. The guys on the sofa sipping Cokes laughed. "You got to pull it all the way out. Pull it halfway and that's as far as it will go." It seemed to be the main topic of conversation there, how you get the Coke machine to work. I went back into my room and fell out on the bed.

After an hour or so I was awakened by my roommate. The lady hadn't told me I was sharing the room. His name was Richard and he had "just come down from Chicago. Been picking bell peppers today," he said, looking nervously at a calendar on the wall that had a picture of a McCormick tractor churning through a field. Last night he'd sat with his uncle who owns the Cities Service station drinking sloe gin till four A.M. and waiting for his aunt to show up. He'd hoped to stay in her trailer but it had turned out she'd sold it. He pulled out the drawers. "Ain't no good magazines here. I left all mine in La Belle. All my clothes too. Ought to be able to catch a ride up there tomorrow.

"I wished it was two months from now," he said, looking back at the calendar. "Two months from now the melons come in. You can make a hundred and ten dollars a day if you know how to pack 'em. They pay twenty-five a trailer. You don't need no social security. No name. No nuthin'.

"I been traveling fifteen years. Been to forty-nine states and four furrin countries. It didn't get me nowhere. Hell, I still ain't nowhere. Well, I decided it was time to stop. Worked in that plastic factory in Chicago, got mad and quit fifteen times. I'm gonna get me a cool beer. Wanna come?"

While a billboard thirty miles east of town proclaims that A WORLD OF OPPORTUNITY AWAITS YOU IN IMMOKALEE, it's liable to be a letdown when you get there and all you find is shacks, shanties, flophouses; trailers where you can get your social security number metal-plated or pictures of yourself blown up into posters; wrestling Tuesday nights at the American Legion; a cluttered thrift shop with JOE SMITH NEW USED ABUSED stenciled in red on the window; and at least twenty bars. "Immokalee is ninety-nine percent niggers and Mexicans," Richard estimated. "The other one percent is Seminoles," he said, giving me a gap-toothed grin.

The year-round population is five thousand. It goes up to twelve or fifteen thousand between October and June, when blacks, Puerto Ricans, and poor whites come in to pick the tomatoes, cukes, bell peppers, and acorn squash. There are also an unknown number of Mexicans, some legal but most without working papers, who hide out in shacks in back of farm fields. The illegals are smuggled in by contractors who promise to pay them at the end of the season; the contractors bring them food, work them, then often turn them over to the border patrol, which flies them back to Mexico from Miami. In April a new, more heavily black contingent comes in to load watermelons. "It's too big a job for wetbacks," Richard explained. The wetbacks tend to stay in Immokalee till school lets out at the end of May, then head up to Ruskin, Florida, with their families to pick tomatoes. Six or seven weeks later they hit the tomatoes in North

Carolina and Virginia, finish up with apples in Illinois and Michigan in September and October, and are back in Immokalee by November. The contractors who intend to pay at all pay cash at the end of every day. A lot of the wages are converted into drink the same night, or laid out at cantinas for expensive cassette tapes of Mexican, country and western, and soul music; Spanish and English sex magazines; and other goods, such as boxes of herbal medicine packaged in Laredo, Texas, by the La India Company: *manzarella* for poor appetite, diarrhea, and headaches; *cuachalate* for making the swelling go down after a baby; *pata vaca* for healing cuts; *diavetina* for diabetes, *eucalipto* for heart disease. By the time they have shelled out for their keep, the crops are in, and the fruit tramps, as they are called, have just enough to make it to the next place.

Richard and I ate a grim New Year's meal of beans and enchiladas at a nameless Mexican restaurant. We were the only gringos in the place. "Peroxide," he confided, motioning with his eyes toward a dumpy blonde chiquita who was wearing a wedding band and didn't look more than fourteen. "They start fucking when they're ten. I'd fuck her for a quarter." On the wall a sign said: *Favor de no desire malas palabras.* and then in English PLEASE DO NOT SAY BAD WORDS IN HERE. A black man sat in the doorway with a transistor radio at his ear, but all we could hear as we stayed there drinking bottle after bottle of brew was a swarm of boat-tailed grackles carrying on in a tree outside. Three police cruisers wailed by, heading, someone guessed, for a fracas at Sam Flint's flophouse. The previous Saturday night there had been four shootings: one killed, two injured, one nicked.

When we got back to our room Hunter, Richard's buddy, was sitting on my bed smoking a cigarette and contemplating the label on his pint of Thunderbird. Richard leaned a chair against the wall and sat there licking the dry saliva from the corners of his mouth and running his tongue over a scar on his upper lip. I asked him what he was thinking about. He said his mother and his old lady, the one he'd been shacking up with since she was sixteen. Now she was thirty-four and her husband was doing twenty years. "So I got plenty of time to worry."

Hunter, a lush, was from Kentucky. "Keep away from this stuff, boy; it'll never let you go," he said, raising the wine to his lips. "I don't know when I got here. I think it was yesterday. I had a good job in Toledo. Machine puncher. Made twenty-five bucks a day. But I got drunk and here I am." Hunter, who had a sad, kind face and a soft, mournful drawl, was now forty-seven. He had been alone and drifting since 1959 when his wife and son were both killed in a car accident. "My other boy ain't quite right. They got him in a state hospital in Raleigh, North Carolina."

I took off my boots and strolled out to the lobby with my guitar. I was pretty smashed myself and bent on having a good time. Just for no reason I started singing an old Carter Family song with a refrain that goes:

> We will all meet again on that great judgment morning.
> The book will be open, the roll will be called.
> Oh how sad it will be if forever we're parted,
> While some rise to glory and others stand to fall.

The doors up and down the hall started opening and about a dozen fruit tramps, their faces lit up with booze and memories, came out to see who was playing the instrument. They started making requests: "Tennessee Waltz," "Pennsylvania Polka," "Wabash Cannonball"; "know any Hank Williams? Gentleman Jim Reeves? Johnny Cash?" I played the ones I knew until the lady came out of the office and said, "If I find one of you drunks out here after midnight I'm going to call the cops."

So we went back into our room and Richard told Hunter and me about how he and his uncle Bert used to go coon hunting. Then they went out and didn't come back till five A.M. I slept through the beginning of the new year, dreaming that the wood storks had come to nest and we were up on the roof putting out grass and balled-up paper in pots for them to build with. "I been two hundred miles," Richard said when he got back. "I been in jail." Later he changed his story to about how he and Hunter had been picked up by the cops and released. "I got a job driving a tractor tomorrow," he informed me. "If I don't work in two days I go crazy. I started picking cotton in Alabama when I was eight." He was gone before I woke up again.

In the morning, New Year's Day, I brushed my teeth at the window as a barefooted Mexican boy outside made figure eights with his bicycle in the dirt, absent-mindedly pulling on a Coke as he rode through his figures. Then I left the flophouse and drove out once more to Corkscrew Swamp.

Halfway down the Audubon Society's boardwalk there is a lake covered solidly with a green mat of water lettuce. I settled in for the morning on a bench overlooking the lake. Twenty feet away a great blue heron stood frozen. He was so absolutely still, so well camouflaged by stillness, that I didn't see him at first. He stood there all morning, intently reading the movements of the lettuce at his feet, sometimes readjusting his head to a new angle, but so slowly I couldn't see it happening. At first I was impressed with his powers

ROYAL ARCH OAK, FLORIDA.

of concentration, but after a while I forgot all about him. So did the fish. Suddenly the heron plunged his head into the leaves and came up with a short-nosed gar, a streamlined predator whose insatiable hunger and nasty teeth were fully evolved sixty million years ago. Gars do their fair share of floating motionless themselves in canals and ditches, waiting for frogs and killifish to let down their guard. The gar was two feet long and would undoubtedly do the heron for a while. Slowly, triumphantly, the bird raised itself on its great blue wings and disappeared around the bend with its catch.

Suddenly I became aware of birds everywhere, their insane laughter, their stock-still stalking, their staccato drumming on trees, their shadows passing over the vegetation. A green heron cackled in a thicket. A red-shouldered hawk screamed *"Kree"* from the tip of a cypress. A white ibis flashed between trunks, its head and neck muddied by feeding. A few feet above me a small, acrobatic blue-gray gnatcatcher snapped at insects. A myrtle warbler darted from one exuberance of plant life to another. It walked confidently on the firm, imbricated mat of azollas, the smallest ferns in the world, floating wetly in the shade; it flew up into the green galleries of pop ash; it began to work the moss-laden branches of pond apple above me. I stared at one of the apple leaves for a while and realized that it was actually the folded wings of a camouflaged butterfly called a ruddy daggerwing. Nearby a pileated woodpecker began digging into an old cypress trunk that had been knocked down by Hurricane Donna on September 10, 1960, and was covered with smilax vines and shriveled resurrection ferns. The woodpecker had braced his stiff tail against the wood, and each time he clubbed it, his red cockade was tossed forward by the impact. At last he threw back his head and let out a satisfied chirp.

Silence came over the lettuce lake, the silence of animals sunning and of leaves soliciting the sunlight: a big mother alligator snoozing in the mud, a languid young cottonmouth draped on a log, a red-bellied turtle, his carapace about as big around as a long-playing record, basking on the lettuce leaves.

A breeze moved in the fireflags, rattling the dry fan leaves of the dead plants. A star-shaped bladderwort, floating in the water, presented a one-way trapdoor to insects. Fresh raccoon scat had been left on the boardwalk. Further down it, two anoles were having a territorial squabble, changing colors from brown to green, depending on which lizard was getting the better of it. I caught a glimpse of an unfamiliar warbler with a red cap and yellow underneath. Suddenly I realized that I wasn't alone. Standing nearby was a radiant, deeply tanned woman with snow-white hair, wearing a flowered purple blouse. She had seen the bird too and told me it was a palm warbler. It turned out that she was the widow of the ornithologist Alexander Sprunt, Jr., who had died a few months before. It was he who had been largely responsible for getting the swamp protected as a sanctuary.

I started up the V–8 engine of my Oldsmobile and prepared for re-entry. The first outpost of civilization I came to was a place called Frank's Truck Stop. Inside, a dozen men were glued to the Cotton Bowl. Frank, the portly proprietor, was lamenting a brilliant run that had just put Penn State ahead of Texas: "The way that little nigger run he must of thought he had a watermelon under his arm." I pulled up a chair with three migrant laborers: a Mexican, a Canadian, and a third man, from Buffalo, New York. Sid, a wetback, had just pulled in from Chicago. It was the Canadian J. W.'s first winter in Florida. He had a farm on Hudson Bay where he grew corn and potatoes in the sixty-day growing season. Mike from Buffalo had been coming to Immokalee for the last ten winters. "When I first come here in sixty-three," he said, "you couldn't walk down the street without a gun in one hand and a knife in another. Now they roll up the streets at six o'clock." Sid, Mike, and J. W. were working a two-hundred-thirty-five-acre farm planted to cukes, tomatoes, and watermelons, bordering Corkscrew Swamp. Dawn to dusk, fourteen bucks a day. And at night they had to stay up in shifts and shoot feral pigs in the melon patch. I asked them if they could use another man. "You can ask the boss," Mike said. We drove down a ground-shell road over a cattle guard, kicking up gray dust. The boss came up on a tractor and told me to grab a can and help the fellers water some new rows of cuke seeds.

"The dumb mother drew the ditches down too low, and now we got to water everything by hand," J. W. complained. Mike dropped a melon into the irrigation ditch to cool off for when we were through. J. W. told me how big his farm was on Hudson Bay. By the end of the day he had it up to fifteen hundred acres. Every hour or so the boss would come over and check up on us. When he was out of earshot the three hirelings would cuss him ritually. They had cussing down to an art. In a month or two, if they didn't get mad and quit before then, they'd be hitching down the road carrying suitcases tied together with string and something strong on their minds, headed for the next crop.

As long as there is water in the ditch and a reservoir of fruit tramps, the banner crops in Immokalee will be grown and shipped north. A circular of the Florida Geological Survey estimates that the five thousand acres of truck farms in the Immokalee area need ten million gallons of water a day. But I could find no information about the effect the ditches have on Corkscrew Swamp, especially on the precarious ecology of the wood stork.

We knocked off at five. I went and drew my pay: six bucks. Mike went back to his wife, who'd made the trip. "My old lady eats like a horse, but she's as skinny as a string bean," he told me. J. W. and Sid patched out for Miami, only forty miles away, in Sid's new Mustang. It was Saturday night, and if the boss wanted somebody to stay and shoot wild hogs he could damn well do it himself. My co-workers had left the watermelon in the ditch, so I reached in and grabbed it. I sat right there watching the sky darken and eating the cool pink fruit. Fifty yards away, three wood storks stood at the water's edge, digesting, their necks drawn in, looking absorbed, for all the world like the members of some religious order.

Sanibel

Down in San Carlos Bay, where the Caloosahatchee empties into the Gulf of Mexico, there's a point called Punta Rasa. Ponce de León was fatally struck by a poisoned dart there in 1521. Today, for three dollars, you can get on a causeway that will take you to two islands, Sanibel and Captiva, which form a twenty-mile crescent at the mouth of the bay. Sanibel's south side faces an eddy of the Gulf Stream and is famous for the shells which litter its shore. On the other side of the island, impounded in the crescent, is a red mangrove swamp, rich in bird life. A subdued resort has grown up on the two islands, drawing people who are more intrigued by birds and shells than by the frivolous glitter of the Gold Coast.

One evening I drove out to the islands. Leaving the car at a lighthouse on the eastern tip of Sanibel, I set out walking down the beach with the full moon at my back, preceded by barely visible hosts of scuttling sanderlings and scaring up huge cormorants, which took off over the waves without a sound. I passed motels, bungalows, condominiums, empty chairs facing the sea, and seagulls, who seemed to have acquired a taste for chlorine, drinking from a swimming pool. A vacationing sophomore from Sarah Lawrence College walked with me for a ways. At one point she clasped her hand to her breast and sighed, "Isn't it soulful?"

A little further on I found some local kids standing around a bonfire on a deserted part of the beach. Among them were Larry and Ronnie Gavin, descendants of freed slaves who homesteaded Sanibel in the last century and became farmers of limes and tomatoes. Theirs is one of the island's oldest and most respected families. All of Larry and Ronnie's eighteen brothers and sisters have left the islands except for a brother who is a carpenter on Captiva and a sister who is a beautician on Sanibel. Larry remembers "when you could count all the people on the islands with your fingers and toes." Also at the bonfire was a girl named Nimmy, who had braces, went to boarding school in North Carolina, and came, as one of the boys told me, from a "mannerly" family. A freak from Chicago was also there, smoking a joint and talking about getting dogs stoned, but nobody was particularly impressed. A lot of cigarette smoking was going on, however. I stayed with the party for an hour or so, then ducked into the Australian pines which line the beach and made myself a pallet with their soft needles. It was early January and the motels were full.

When I woke up, I had a view of the sea through the trees, spread out in bands of green, purple, green, purple, green, and purple unbroken to the horizon. The tide was out and had left sea slugs and Portuguese men-of-war heaving on the beach. A Louisiana blue heron stepped judiciously along the edge of an inlet, his claw closing as he picked up a foot, and opening as he set it down again. His wispy white mane was flapping in the breeze. The fin of a dolphin broke

Florida's Famed Health Spa

WARM MINERAL SPRINGS

"THE REAL FOUNTAIN OF YOUTH"
VENICE, FLORIDA

the surface just a dozen yards from shore. A tern wheeling overhead just stopped flying and let himself drop out of the air, steering headfirst into the water on radically tilted wings. A speedy pack of sandpipers skimmed the water, traveling a route of frantic angles. A fisherman, standing in a small outboard, whose hull was draped with nets, cut across the outermost band of purple. Long after he had passed, his wake kept coming ashore.

I probably could have walked out to the final purple band—a quarter of a mile or so—without getting my hair wet. From the edge of the Gulf Coast, the continental shelf continues for a hundred miles, but thirty miles offshore it is still only fifty feet deep. This area —flat, stable, sheltered, enriched by the Caloosahatchee River and by the tons of nutrients that the Mississippi pours into the Gulf of Mexico—is solidly encrusted with mollusk beds. The free-swimming larval stages of some tropical mollusks drift up from the West Indies on the Gulf Stream, but not many of these survive in the colder water except on salt domes far out on the submarine plateau. So most of the shellfish that wash up on Sanibel are ones that inhabit the Carolinian province of shellfish, which goes from North Carolina to the tip of Florida. A good norther can churn up shells buried a foot deep and blow them ashore by the millions with the animals still in them. The birds have a field day. These deposits are known as "windfalls."

Every seven years or so billions of shellfish living in the shallows are purged by a mysterious epidemic known as red tide. In July of 1971 blood-red patches were noticed on the water. Fish began to die by the ton; then oysters, clams, and other mollusks washed up on the beaches of Sanibel, poisoned by massive blooms of one of the one-cell marine plant-animals known as a dinoflagellates. The smell of rotten fish lingered for weeks, making the area repellent to boaters, beachcombers, and sunbathers. Sixteen major red tides have struck the Gulf Coast of Florida since 1844. What triggers off the blooms isn't exactly known, but among the necessary conditions appear to be the right admixture of fresh water from rivers, rain, or sewage outlets; the right amounts of nutrients and trace metals; the right temperature and salinity; strong sunlight and calm weather; and the presence of tannic acid, which is brought into the Gulf by flood-swollen rivers. Some blame the epidemic on the increasing amounts of nutrients that are being dumped into the ocean by rivers polluted with sewage and agricultural runoff. But the fact is that this red-tide business has been going on for centuries in other parts of the world where the word "pollution" hasn't yet entered the local vocabulary.

On this fine morning, though, there were no poisoned mollusks on Sanibel, only beautiful shells. People were picking over them and making off with sunrise tellins, turkey wings, pens, starfish, Great Atlantic cockles, Vanhyning's cockles, lady's toenails, moon snails, leafy jewel boxes, olives, figs, tulip conchs, Florida fighting conchs, lightning whelks, turnip whelks, slipper shells, buttercups, and ponderous arks, which make up ninety-five percent of the deposits. Shells were everywhere. The whole island, as a matter of fact, consists of a milky sand of ground-up shells spread over a foundation of Pliocene and Pleistocene limestones. From a distance, the beach seems pure calcitic white. On closer inspection the shells turn out to be flecked with red, purple, orange, yellow, brown, black, and occasionally green. This morning two lines of red algae marked recent high tides. Jumbled in with the seaweed were mangrove leaves, a willet's feather, a long string of whelk egg sacs, and some tough gelatinous brown lumps, but no one on the beach could tell me what they were. Where the waves still reached, the sand was streaked with black organic ooze. Each wave, as it receded, left a sheen of wetness sinking into the sand.

I had breakfast at the Coral Gables Restaurant in the island's only shopping center. An old Greek with white mustaches named Continas came in with a basket of hibiscus blossoms and gave one to the waitress Marianne, who wore a Mickey Mouse ring and a Vietnam prisoner-of-war bracelet. Marianne brought another cup of coffee to a man at the counter who seemed to be hung over. His name was Abrams and he was involved in the development of the island that had followed the construction of the causeway in 1963. Abrams was bitterly against conservation. "Man is part of the ecology. I don't think it's right to let land lie unused. What good does it do anybody?" In a rack near the door there was a pamphlet called *How to Buy Florida*. It had questions about a development further up the coast called Punta Gorda Isles.

Q. Is there good t.v. reception in the area? . . .

Q. Does Punta Gorda Isles have paved streets?

A. Yes, the finest asphalt paved streets, and engineered drainage as a high quality home community should. This means the developer has spent roughly $200.00 for each homesite to give you this necessary all-important physical improvement, and this has been included in the purchase price.

Q. Where do I dock my boat? . . .

I gave a call to Mike Dormer, one of the boys I had met at the beach party, to see if he still felt like sailing. "Shore, I'll take you out," he said. "Got nothin' else to do." We met up at his house at the end of a ground-shell road which put a hole in one of my tires.

After changing it we loaded his dingy on my convertible and headed for the water. First, though, we stopped at a Caloosa Indian shell mound from about A.D. 100, covered over with morning-glory vines and a copse of gumbo-limbo trees. Among the shells were occasional shards of sand-baked pottery and whole "implement shells," conchs with holes bored into them to fit a handle through. The mound was soon to be bulldozed into a housing project, Mike told me, "as if it had no history." Nearby we found an old brown bottle that said "The Great Dr. Kilmer's Swamp Root Kidney Liver and Bladder Cure—Specific. Binghamton, New York." Mike is nearly twenty. A junior at the University of Florida, he lives in Gainesville in a complex of two-story modern apartments called La Bonne Vie, which has its own pool. He plays bass in a band that is highly influenced by the Allman Brothers, and he wants to go into the foreign service.

From the shell mound Mike and I continued to the J. N. "Ding" Darling National Wildlife Refuge, a four-thousand-acre tract of mangrove swamp and estuarine bottomland on the island's impounded north side, which was brought under protection through the actions of a well-known thirties cartoonist. We put the dingy into a shallow bay surrounded by mangrove islands, which were suspended several feet above the tide by their prop roots. For hours we glided back and forth between their lee and windward sides, not that it made much difference. "When we round this island, we're going to take off," Mike kept promising. But nothing of the sort happened. Our transition from one tack to another was more often assisted by the timely insertion of an oar. The sun beat down mercilessly. "I don't see any birds," Mike said. "They must be goofing off in the mangroves." We peered into the labyrinthine interior of one of the islets. Mike let out a low whistle. "Ain't that a growth in there!"

Whole sections of branches and leaves were coated white with droppings, but we saw no birds. "See those branches going into the water? They're forming roots. Sand and all kinds of stuff collects around them. That's how you get land." Clusters of oysters were clinging to some of the prop roots too. "Used to be you could eat 'em, but being stationary, they're more subject to pollution."

At last we saw a bird, a yellow-crowned night heron standing inert in the water. His brown eyes bulged as we passed. Three mullet jumped, maybe to itch their backs, to shake off a predator, or just because they felt like a change of element. "Hey, there go a couple of ibis." The birds were beginning to come out now. A little blue heron flapped past with his neck tucked in. Way above us, an osprey, or sea eagle, hovered in place. We found his mate several islets later at a nest that looked like a big wicker basket. She was cackling exultantly over a sea trout she had draped over a dead branch. Mike told me that in the early days of Sanibel ospreys used to nest on people's roofs. They made fine watchdogs. Whenever a stranger approached they would let out a piercing shriek. They could spot someone coming a mile away.

Rounding another islet we came upon a group of roseate spoonbills feeding in a mud flat. They were doing exactly what Audubon had described them as doing a hundred and forty years ago:

To procure their food, the Spoonbills first generally alight near the water, into which they then wade up to the tibia, and immerse their bills in the water or soft mud, sometimes with the head and even the whole neck beneath the surface. They frequently withdraw these parts, however, and look around to ascertain if danger is near. They move their partially opened mandibles laterally to and fro with a considerable degree of elegance, munching the fry, insects, or small shell-fish, which they secure, before swallowing them. When there are many together, one usually acts as sentinel, unless a Heron should be near; and in either case you may despair of approaching them.

Sure enough, we came too close, and just as Audubon had said would happen, one of them sounded the alarm by uttering "a grunting croak in a low key and so subdued as not to be audible at any great distance," and they all took off together, their necks and legs stretched out to form a single line, higher and higher, until the ten rich bits of pink were only specks in the vastness of the sky. They were the first spoonbills I had ever seen. Still other birds took to the air as a wave of fright spread over the mudflat: blue-winged teal, shovelers, and pintails who had been chasing minnows toward the shores into the waiting gullets of herons and ibises hurled themselves vertically out of the water. A group of canvasbacks kicked along just above the surface until they gathered enough speed to become airborne. Through field glasses, we saw, way out, a skimmer shearing water with its long lower mandible, and a reddish egret who had apparently strayed across the Gulf from Texas, striding across the flat with its wings flared out, herding minnows past a motionless black-crowned night heron. This spectacle is known as canopy feeding.

Behind the egret we saw a stunning and outrageous creature that looked like, and was, a flamingo. It was constantly shuffling its long, rickety legs, as if to keep warm. Its flame-red neck, even longer than its legs, stretched into the muddy water. Every so often it would come up and give a quick look around. This one bird was first sighted at Sanibel in 1971. It has no mate and keeps to itself. For some reason it is estranged from the forty or fifty other wild flamingoes on the continent, who stay at Cape Sable in Florida Bay. Watching it, we forgot about ourselves, sitting motionless until the wind finally made us aware of our tight red skin, coated like the mangrove leaves with a fine layer of salt, and we realized it was time to come about.

Indians and Airboats

The moon was gibbous on the Tamiami Trail as I cruised through the din of millions of frogs which would die out suddenly and start up again moments later. Red veins of lightning stood out on the horizon and lit the edges of the rolling thunderheads that hang over the Everglades all summer long. At this time of year, usually from June to October, the whole interior of the peninsula, from Lake Okeechobee south, is flooded with a vast sheet of water that appears to be standing in the saw grass, but is actually creeping toward the sea at the rate of half a mile per day. The seaward tilt of the basin is barely perceptible, only two inches per mile, and the only limits to the amount of sky you can take in at one time are your own peripheral vision, and the mountains of cloud that block the horizon.

This may well be the most mosquito-plagued stretch of fresh water in the world. First you must contend with the glades mosquito, a smaller and fiercer relative of the common house mosquito. According to one conscientious government survey, there are thirteen of these little buggers for every cubic inch of atmosphere. You are also at the mercy of sandflies, or no-see-ums, who can penetrate the finest mesh of mosquito netting. They become active at sunset, and there is a slight delay before the allergic reaction to their injected saliva registers with your nervous system, so by the time you become aware that one has bitten you, it is usually chewing on some other part of your body. Finally, there are the abominable red bugs or "chiggers" of the South, which get under your skin and raise welts around your waist and along the edge of your socks.

I began to realize that the river of grass was not so monotonous as it at first seemed. In places, pieces of limestone crust, littered with the empty shells of apple snails left there by limpkins, stood in glittering pools. In other places the saw grass was dense, eight to ten feet tall, and obscured the water. Elsewhere cypress saplings were scattered on the prairie and seemed to be pioneering its transition into a swamp.

I was so absorbed in discovering these variations that I didn't see the black screen of rain moving quickly across the grass like a squall line over troubled waves. The next thing I knew I was in a blinding tropical downpour. It was beyond anything I'd ever experienced. On my left I could barely make out a stockadelike enclosure with a sign that said BIG CYPRESS BEND INDIAN VILLAGE. Then three things happened in rapid succession: my Oldsmobile conked out, a lightning bolt slammed into a telephone pole fifty feet away, and I got out and made a run for the stockade. Great balls of fire! The air reeked of ozone and sizzling wood. There was enough electricity around to raise the hair on my arm. The stockade gate was bolted from within. I went around to the back and knocked on the plywood door of a small hut. After a moment's delay, it was opened by an eight-year-old Indian girl in her nightgown. Inside a man named Bobby Henry and his wife sat in bed watching *To Tell the Truth* on a small blue television set. Their other daughter lay on a platform under a stack of quilts, staring up at me. The roof of the hut was made of thatched palm fronds, and it leaked. The major leaks were being caught in pots and jars. Smaller trickles splattered on the floor.

"Roof's ten years old," said Bobby Henry, grinning. "Not much good any more. Guess it's gettin' time to make a new one." Then he said something to his older daughter in a language called Eela-ponke, a word which means literally "mother tongue." She brought me a chair. Bobby Henry works in Naples for a septic-tank outfit. Work was slow. Everything gets washed out in the rains this time of year. Cloudbursts occur daily, dumping inches in a matter of minutes.

In one corner was an electric sewing machine. Sewing machines were eagerly adopted by the Indians of the Everglades at the turn of the century: first hand-cranked ones, then the foot-powered treadle type, and now electrics where the power is hooked in. Televisions, cars, and airboats are now also in general use. The eighty-eight families, or four hundred and eighty-six souls, who make up the Miccosuki tribe, have, until recently, shown little interest in the other devices of modern technology.

Originally the Miccosukis, hunters, gatherers, fishermen, were part of the Creek nation. They ranged through Georgia and the Carolinas, but were forced southward as the white man displaced them from their land. There they intermarried with the Seminoles, who had also been pushed down from the North, and with the indigenous tribes of Florida, some of whom were cannibals: the Timucua, the Tequesta, the Apalachee, and the Caloosa. They also welcomed slaves who had been brought over from Africa, especially from among warlike tribes like the Ibo and Egba, the Senegalese from Dakar, and the Ashanti from the Gold Coast. In time the white man became interested in Florida. During the first half of the nineteenth century the U.S. Army made repeated attempts to eradicate "the savages," but without noteworthy success. Finally, however, the Army's persistence yielded results, and in 1868 most of the troublesome aborigines surrendered and agreed to move to Indian Territory in Oklahoma, where fifty years later they struck oil. Some of them became millionaires.

But two hundred of the proudest and orneriest of the Miccosukis stayed holed up in the Everglades, preferring to adjust to a prairie that is stinging with life and under water half the time, than to fall in with the civilization that was overrunning the continent. They gave up their buckskin pants and coats for bright calico kilts, lighter and better suited for wading. They turned from log huts to open-air "chickees"—simple structures consisting of thatched roofs supported by posts and containing living platforms to keep off invasion by water and animals. They hewed dugouts from cypress logs and fitted them with masts and sails. For years their wilderness existence was disturbed only by missionaries, bootleggers, and alligator poachers. That isolation ended in 1928, though, when the Tamiami Trail, a new, modern highway connecting Tampa and Miami, was completed across the Everglades. Soon the Miccosukis began to run into fences in places they had always been able to walk straight across before. It was explained to them that now they were in Conservation Area Three of the Central and Southern Flood Control District and that they could hunt, fish, and farm only in the eighty-seven thousand acres north of the Tamiami Trail. They began to understand the meaning of these words as members of the tribe were pistol-whipped for trespassing, and as flood canals gradually lowered the water level of the river of grass, until by the 1950s it was no longer possible to live off the land. Most of the Miccosukis hunkered down in chickees along the Tamiami Trail and made a living by wrestling alligators for tourists, giving airboat rides, and selling mock-Indian artifacts.

Finally, a white woman named Laverne Madigan, who headed the Association on American Indian Affairs, advised the Miccosukis to draw up a constitution and enter into relations with the United States, which they had never recognized. In 1962 the Department of the Interior formally acknowledged that they were a tribe, and as the crowning gesture of mutual recognition, in 1964 the Miccosukis sent their tribal chairman Buffalo Tiger and assistant chairman Sonny Billy to President Johnson's inauguration. But, to this day, only half of the Miccosukis are enrolled in the tribe. The rest of them, including Bobby Henry and his family, don't see the point of it.

No wonder Bobby Henry's wife and children didn't have much to say to the strange white hombre who had busted into their hut, dripping wet. Occasionally one of them would mutter something in Eelaponke. I couldn't tell if it was about me or about what was happening on *To Tell the Truth*, but it would always set them off giggling for the better part of a minute. Between bouts of laughter their faces would settle into a look of dead seriousness. The leaks grew feeble, and finally petered out completely. Bobby Henry went out with me to his Chevy truck and got my car started with jumper cables. I hopped in, tendered my thanks, and drove on. Finally, just beat, I parked behind a gas station, and spent the night in the car fighting off chiggers, no-see-ums, and glades mosquitoes.

Next morning I was back on the Trail, driving past Miccosuki

Miami, Fla.   Seminole Indians.

camps; past a group of women and children pounding wash in the canal that lines the road and spreading it to dry in the low button-bushes; past a flotilla of gallinules and coots; past a billboard that said ALLIGATOR WRESTLING DAILY; past an anhinga drying his wings and rhythmically undulating his neck, for which habit he is also called the snakebird; past an old black man slumped in a collapsible deck chair over a long cane fishing pole. Suddenly I came to a barren clearing where the prairie had been smothered with fill and criss-crossed with runways. To one side, perched crazily on the roof of a building, a rusty four-engine Stratocruiser loomed, the whole thing looking like nothing so much as a gigantic bowling trophy. This was the abandoned passenger-arrivals building of the uncompleted Big Cypress Swamp Jetport. The project, begun in 1968, galvanized the conservation movement in South Florida, which managed to stop it two years later. Its success would have spelled ruin for the Miccosukis and their home.

Several miles further down the trail I came across the Miccosuki Restaurant. I pulled into the parking lot in front of it and slipped the Olds neatly between two pickups whose plates said, "Miccosuki Indian." As a special favor, the state of Florida lets its native Americans register their vehicles for free. Inside the restaurant the atmosphere was cool and Polynesian. A long-haired brave in a football shirt was beating out with his hands on top of a jukebox the tempo of a country and western forty-five. His name was Duane Billy, and he worked as a janitor at a school attended by forty-two Miccosukis between the ages of five and fourteen. Duane looked much younger than twenty-five. Unlike Bobby Henry, who seemed more at home in Eelaponke, he spoke English fluently and with beautiful softness. "The older you get," he told me, "the more important you realize it is that you're an Indian." There was something incredibly open and vulnerable about him. "If I learn just the white people's way I might get hurt. The Indian way is what God tell you." I took a seat at a picture window. A large-hipped waitress in a patchwork skirt rustled up to me with the menu. The specialty de la maison was deep-fried frog legs. Frogging is one of the tribe's main sources of income, as gourmet restaurants in Miami pay $1.25 a pound and more for frog legs. The Miccosukis themselves turn green at the thought of eating frogs, even though assured they taste a whole lot like chicken.

I struck up a conversation with Charlie Sanford, deputy sheriff of Collier County, who was in for a cup of coffee. Charlie is an old friend of the tribe, and, like them, is upset by the changes that the Everglades have seen in the last decade. He said that thousands of migrating curlews used to stop on his lawn each spring. "Haven't seen a one of 'em for three years now." On the bright side, though, it looked like the alligators have been coming back strong since they became federally protected in 1969. On cloudy days they like to lie on the road, and the sheriff had been having to stop his car and nudge six- and seven-footers back into the canal.

"Lookie there," he said. Through the window we saw a dusky black bird of prey with red face and legs, poised on a slender poke-weed plant, making it teeter back and forth like a metronome. Suddenly the bird squirted a thin white line of excrement and took off cruising, volplaning, intently scrutinizing the saw grass. "That's an Everglades kite. You don't know how lucky you are to see one. There's only thirty-two of them left." These birds are in the same position as whooping cranes, ivory-billed woodpeckers, and California condors. The reason they're so rare is that each kite requires at least three dozen apple snails a day. A combination of natural drought and artificial drainage has created a shortage of the mollusks in the Everglades. Limpkins and boat-tailed grackles have first crack at what snails there are.

On the canal behind the restaurant floated an open flat-bottom boat that drew only a couple of inches. Its hull was made of riveted sheets of aircraft aluminum and toward the stern, bolted to a cypress frame and mounted on thick metal braces, was an exposed airplane motor. Over the carburetor, feeding the engine by gravity pull, was a small gas tank. And behind the engine was a two-blade pusher propeller encased in a circular metal cage like a big fan. Finally, behind the propeller was a rectangular, vertically hinged rudder. Over the rudder a sign said TIGER'S AIRBOATS. At the bow, in the driver's seat, was a very fat young man wearing mirror shades and reading a hotrod magazine. His name was Howard Billy. I asked him if he felt like taking me for a spin on the saw grass. He said I could have the short ride for four bucks and the long one for eight. If I took the long one I would get to see a real Indian camp deep in the Everglades. That was fine by me.

Billy went back to the propeller and gave it a turn. The infernal racket of the uncovered engine started up a few feet from our ears. Further conversation was out of the question. Howard got back in the driver's seat and stepped on a foot-operated accelerator. That was the only control, other than a stick he gripped in his left hand to move the rudder back and forth. There were no brakes, keel, or reverse. You stopped by decelerating and executing a quick ninety-degree turn, like a hockey player does on skates.

We took off up a channel that cut straight up the interminable morass as far as I could see. Although we were skimming the water only lightly, we pushed big waves into the saw grass. Ten minutes later we put into a small dock on a tree island, also known as a "bayhead," or simply a "head," and in Eelaponke as a *kantakle*. This *kantakle* was less than an acre and shaped like a teardrop with its blunt end toward the current. The center of it had been cleared to allow space for a garden, several fruit trees, a lawn, and two chickees. A man named Tommy Tiger, his wife, and the last of their twelve children live on it. The rest are grown up. Tommy Tiger is an older brother of Buffalo Tiger, the tribal chairman. He was sitting in a pile of shavings against a tree with blue fruit he called a *negagi* and for which he didn't know the English, whittling a souvenir knife from a cypress sapling. He was wearing black leather shoes, no socks, a hard straw cowboy hat, and a patchwork shirt which his wife had sewn together from bright bits of calico, gingham, cotton, and flannel. His wife was sitting on a platform under one of the chickees, piecing together another shirt with a sewing machine. She had on a long dress. "My daughters wear shorts and miniskirts, but I don't want people to see my legs," she explained. She wore the traditional twenty or thirty pounds of beads around her neck, threaded on separate strands. She had received these for birthdays and earned them for acts of virtue. Later in her life she would begin to give the strands away one by one until only the first one remained. This she would wear to the grave. She wore her long black hair tucked behind an upright cardboard visor inside a net of woven black thread in a style called the "pompadour hairdo," which the Seminoles and Moccosukis had adopted from the Gibson Girls' look of the 1890s.

Under the thatched roof of the second chickee a blackened cast-iron pot hung over the smoldering ends of four logs which had been laid to point in the directions of the compass. Tommy's wife sits on one of the logs when she cooks. When the fire has to be stoked, she just gets up and slides the log ends in closer toward the center. She keeps the pot warm all the time and always has something in it, because the Tigers aren't into the routine of three meals a day, but eat Indian style, whenever they're hungry. In one corner of the chickee was a mortar and pestle made of cypress and used for grinding corn to produce a fermented beverage called *safki*. Pumpkins, potatoes, and corn were in the garden, cocoa plum and starchy-rooted elephant ears in the water. Tommy had planted guava, papaya, and lemon trees on the lawn, along with a patch of mint which his wife uses to flavor her fish and turtle stew. The grass is kept under control by a combination of marsh rabbits and a hand lawnmower which Tommy brought to the island. Tommy does not own a watch.

The Tigers are the largest Miccosuki family, and they are pretty much in charge of things. The clan is named for the Florida panther, a close relative of the western mountain lion; a few still roam the Everglades, but they are hardly ever seen. Tommy's younger brother, Buffalo, the tribal chairman, is a busy man, commuting between an office in Hialeah and one on the Tamiami Trail. He has two white girls fielding his phone calls and answering his correspondence. Lately Buffalo has been involved with plans for developing the 120,000-acre reservation in Broward County that is jointly used by the Miccosukis and the Seminoles. He wants a hotel there, and a souvenir and sandwich shop. No Miccosukis live on the reservation. It is leased to cattle ranchers for pasture and to Exxon, which is exploring it for oil. These leasing transactions and frogging bring in most of the tribe's income. Ninety-four percent of its employable members are below federal poverty standards of $3,600 annual income for a family of three. Once a year each member of the tribe gets a dividend check, which is never more than a few hundred dollars.

Unlike Tommy Tiger, Buffalo believes that the old way of life has been defeated by white man's progress, and that "we got to face the problem and adjust ourselves." In keeping with his philosophy, he wears modern clothes: a paisley cowboy shirt, a string tie, a tooled leather belt, slim slacks. Another Tiger brother, whom I did not meet, wrestles alligators for a living. I was told that he had recently come out of one match minus a finger. Then there is a sister, Annie Mae Jim, whom I met at the Ross Allen Reptile Institute in Silver Springs, where she and her mother-in-law, Annie Jim, receive a small daily sum simply for their presence. Annie Mae Jim is married to a Seminole and does not consider herself a Miccosuki any more.

I found still a fourth Tiger brother, Jimmy, in his souvenir store across the street from the Miccosuki Restaurant. Jimmy is a tall, dignified man with long, straight silver hair. He had on a beautiful patchwork jacket, a black scarf tied around his neck, and gray pants. I asked him what he thought about airboats. "Somebody cut down the trees. Willows have grown up all over the place. We can't get around in canoes any more, so we got to use airboats. Airboats go running in where people never been before. Kill everything. Just for fun. Airboats ruin the state of Florida." He picked up a bag of salt-water toffee from a tray and flung it down again.

Many of the people Jimmy complained about belong to the Airboaters' Association of Florida, whose headquarters is just two miles down the road from his store. I dropped by there late that afternoon. There were several dozen of the contraptions around the caretaker's house, mounted on fiberglass or aluminum bodies. Some were powered by rebuilt Buick, Ford V–8, and Volkswagen engines. They

D. C. 58—Seminole Indians
Wrestling Alligators at Musa Isle,
Miami, Fla.

MUSA ISLE
INDIAN VILLAGE

had names like *Hurricane* and *The Gator*. One was big enough to carry twenty people.

"What do you use 'em for?" I asked the caretaker.

"You use 'em in shallow water where you can't get nuthin' else. Used to be you could go clear from Lake Okeechobee to the ocean, but the National Park won't let 'em in any more so they can only operate in Flood Control Districts 3–A and 3–B. You use 'em for pleasure, hunting, and covering ground to your camps."

One of the Association's three hundred and fifty members, who has an airboat store in Hialeah, joined the conversation. "I got letters from Alaska," he said. "They're using 'em on the ice and snow. You can run 'em right over yer lawn early in the morning, before the dew burns off. We had eight airboat parties last week flushed deer out of the hammocks. If the deer's got horns on him, you shoot him." But wasn't deer season four months away? "Yeah, but we was just getting the dogs ready for it." He asked me if I cared for a beer.

The airboat was invented in the twenties by a stunt man named Hubert Richmond. It is used by wardens of the Florida Game and Fish Commission and also by alligator poachers, who drop the weighted carcasses over the side and tear out in special high-speed rigs if they are surprised by the law. When a Lockheed 1011 Tristan jumbo jet careered into the Everglades on December 29, 1972, airboats were instrumental in the recovery operation. "They also use 'em for commercial froggin'," the caretaker said. "They frog off 'em at night. Cruise at fifteen, twenty mile an hour, shine 'em up with a headlamp, and spear 'em with a four-pronged spear."

"We also race 'em," the man from Hialeah butted in again. "One of 'em went airborne last week. Hit a clump of grass. Driver lost his hand." Then he took me for a spin in his one-man modified racing rig. We barrelassed across the prairie with me huddled in the space between his legs, my eyeballs two feet from the ground literally bulging as rapierlike blades of saw grass were mowed down right in front of them. On the way back we hit ninety, and though I'd been faster in my convertible, it was the fastest my stomach had ever gone, and the fastest it ever cared to go, thankyou.

The Panhandle

Like a good reporter I blew into Tallahassee and poked around in a few bureaucratic drawers. Outside of the fancy new bank, the Larsen building, and a few other modern buildings, the slumbrous antebellum flavor of the capital seems pretty much intact. "Jess don't forgit to set yer watch back thirty years," the one-armed D-Day veteran who took the keys to my convertible ribbed me. I had studiously acquired what I had thought to be the proper uniform for the purpose of sleuthing around the capital, a baggy old seersucker suit, but it turned out that everybody there wears creaseproof nylon knits these days. Most of the new breed didn't have time for an itinerant young journalist whose duds were wrinkled and outmoded. I was given a hearty welcome, though, by the man in charge of the biological control of waterweeds, and by two of his colleagues in the departments of chemical and mechanical waterweed management. It was probably the first time a member of the fourth estate had ever paid them a visit.

One afternoon I sat in on a subcommittee hearing in which a Gulf Coast developer was being investigated for illegal dredging. I couldn't help feeling sorry for the poor man as he sat there fidgeting with his ballpoint pen. He had been caught in changing times, and some of the committeemen who were holding him to the new laws protecting the shoreline were the same people who had thought well of his blueprints five years earlier. After the hearing I went back to where I was camping and waded through the reams of printed matter I'd collected in Tallahassee. My camp was located up a deserted logging road strewn with rusty cans. I kept expecting to run into a hobo or to be beaten up by rednecks, as any well-brought-up Northerner believes is supposed to happen in the South. The only thing that disturbed my solitude, though, was the power-generating plant for the city of Tallahassee, which put on a sensational light show all night long in the neighboring field, I assume for the benefit of low-flying aircraft. At one point I strolled over into the field and came across a large green moth with swallowtails, flying sideways in wide arcs. It was a luna moth, the first one I'd ever seen alive; they're as rare as a blue moon nowadays. All the silk moths have been decimated by pesticides. The magnificent cecropia, which I saw once on a porch screen in the Adirondacks when I was a boy, has also practically disappeared. I crawled under my mosquito netting and lay there, glad to know a few of the good moths are still around.

As the light of day poured in through the trees I could just make out the redness of a cardinal skipping from branch to branch. I found a batch of honey mushrooms, *Armillaria mellea,* fastened to the root of an oak tree, and cooked them up in the kitchen I was running out of the trunk of the car. First I parboiled them to take away their bitterness, then fried them in butter on a low flame. Then, for the price of a few scratches, I followed them up with an order of blackberries. The day was off to a good start.

Heading west I soon left greater Tallahassee behind me and entered the realm of yellow pine which takes up most of the Panhandle. For a long time there was no break in the wispy plumes of slash and loblolly pine, except for one sign that said TREES GROW JOBS. Suddenly I broke into a sunlit clearing where a group of black people had just stepped out of the small white-steepled Hacklebarney Baptist Church, and were shaking hands and walking to their cars. Then there was nothing but the lonesome flatwoods again, mitigated only by a series of signs spaced at five-mile intervals. They said:

REPENT THAT YOUR SINS MAY BE BLOTTED OUT

REPENT IT IS GOD'S COMMAND
DON'T DEFY GOD IN YOUR PRIDE

WE MAY ENTER THE KINGDOM OF GOD
BY THE BLOOD OF JESUS (NO OTHER WAY)

FEAR GOD WHO HAS POWER
TO CAST INTO HELL FIRE

(Little red flames coursed along the bottom of the last one.)

I passed an old lady with long blond hair in a ponytail, riding a pony; a big pile of red sawdust; a rustic drive-in whose bill of fare was *Tarzana the Wild Girl, Dead, Dead Delilah,* and *Terror in the Jungle;* a burly man emerging from a trailer, his beet-red belly hanging over his jeans; a Tennessee blue-tick coon hound sprawled out in front of him; two more hound dogs barking at each other through either end of a culvert, their tails a-wag. I pulled up to a small ramshackle gas station to investigate a sign that said COLD CANE JUICE. Zeke Smith, prop., a very fat man, was sitting out front. Sticking out of his pocket was a flashlight that was on. He explained in a slow, thick drawl that he was temporarily out of cane juice but was expecting some more later in the day. Inside his office, hanging from the ceiling, was an old Ford steering wheel with a sign under it that said, "This steering wheel is for rent by the hour or day." A German shepherd named Lady lay in the corner on a chain. "Make friends with him," Zeke ordered, and Lady jumped up on me, tail wagging. "Give him a paw." Lady did so. Then he told me to stand back and said to the dog, "Keep an eye on him," and Lady curled up her lip and growled. Then he said, "Show him who's boss," and Lady shrank into the corner. Then he took a big, round cookie out of a glass jar and threw it to Lady, who caught it in her mouth and began to eat it. When she was halfway through the cookie he told her to "spit it out," and she did. "I could make her stop eating a steak if I wanted to," Zeke informed me.

Further on, I bought red potatoes from a wild-eyed man in a straw hat who asked me if I was a Christian, then I wandered over to examine a wider selection of roadside produce across the street. A boy who couldn't have been more than ten kept quoting outrageous prices for whatever I picked up. His eyes, sunk deep in his head, avoided me. I let it ride and bought a tomato for fifty cents.

The road went over a creek that had no name. It was running fast, stained pitch-black by bark, roots, and leaves. Not knowing how deep it was, cautiously, feet first, I dropped in from the bank. With the water just above my knees I hit clean white sand. Two densely freckled boys in inner tubes drifted by, trolling worms from fishing poles, on their way to Telogia, eight miles down. Gray bark mantises

WINTER SHUFFLE BOARD, THE PALM BEACHES, FLORIDA—K1

clung to water oaks and hickories along the bank.

Just east of the Apalachicola River I came to the sizable community of Bristol. It has a grass strip, long enough to land Cessna bush planes, which are used by hunters, doctors, and firefighters in the State Forest Service. The Apalachee Restaurant, where I had lunch, served up three farm-grown catfish smothered with French fries and four little hush puppies on the edge of the plate. There is a motel in Bristol run by a man who also manages the career of Tammy Wynette, a big singer in Nashville. There are, as well, several gas stations and package stores. Bristol is the only place in the world where *Torreya taxifolia,* known locally as the gopherwood tree, grows and is also the home of a man named Elvy E. Callaway, who contends that the town is the exact location of the original Garden of Eden. After polishing off my catfish, I dropped in on the lanky eighty-four-year-old fundamentalist. He was sitting in a wicker rocker in the middle of his wood-paneled living room, smoking down a cigar butt in his pipe, scarcely two hundred yards from the spot where there is no doubt in his mind God created Adam. He had on two layers of checkered work shirt, one blue and black, the other red and gray. His white mustache was thin and meticulously trimmed. Three moles had just been removed from his left temple, leaving a vertical row of stitches. There was a white halo around his chin. He hadn't shaved that day.

Callaway's convictions are founded on the "great vegetative similarities" between the Garden of Eden as the Bible describes it and the Apalachicola River Valley. According to him, twenty-seven out of the twenty-eight species of trees that are named in the Bible have been found here. In particular he points to Bristol's unique gopherwood tree, from which the Bible says Noah fashioned the ark. Then there is the matter of Genesis, chapter 2, verse 10, which Callaway has committed to memory: "And a river went out of Eden to water the garden; and from thence it was parted, and became into four heads."

"Now, the Apalachicola River," he explained, "which is formed by the confluence of the Chattahoochee, Fish Pond Creek, Spring Creek, and the Flint, is the only four-head river system in the world. It's true there is one lake in the center of Russia that is the source of four small rivers, and some people have tried to tie down that area as the Garden of Eden. Not a scintilla of evidence to support it." He spoke his case well, as a man who had practiced law for over fifty years, who'd been born, as he phrased it, "under a veil" in a log house in Alabama, educated himself from the Bible and the Harvard Classics, made a fortune in Lakeland in the boom twenties, toured the state with William Jennings Bryan to raise funds for the University of Florida, run for Governor on the Republican ticket of 1934 and lost, and finally retired to Bristol in 1947 on "a suspicion of t.b."

"The facts are beyond intelligent contradiction," he concluded. "They speak for themselves. They are *res ipsa loquitur.*" Then he expanded the discussion to two favorite subjects, "that infamous system of progressive education," and the theory of evolution, to which he does not adhere.

Callaway recommended a visit to Torreya State Park, a few miles north of Bristol on the eastern bluffs of the Apalachicola. There, he said, I would find some deep "glens and dells" at whose heads springs gurgle out with "as fine water as there is on earth." On one of the bluffs, commanding a fine view of the river, is a Greek Revival plantation house that was moved there from the other bank some thirty years ago to become the park headquarters.

Over at the park I met a man sitting in the shadow of a tool shed, who had on the gray uniform of the Park Service, and a straw hat, dyed gray. His name was Roy Clay. "Jes' remember, a little bit of sand, and a little bit of mud, and you got muh name." Roy's thick lips creased into a broad smile. A hundred feet below us the river glided by, carrying all sorts of debris: branches, the hood of a car, the roof of a shack. It was glassy and quiet except where the water was strained by a snag. On its bank were heaps of empty moon snails, clams, and oysters that had been pried open by coons. Wintering warblers darted among the moss-hung branches along its bank. There is also a flock of wild turkeys, to whom Roy Clay feeds chicken scratch at the end of every day.

The river was muddy brown, the color of the alluvial clay it washes down from Georgia. On the west bank, several hundred yards away, tons of the "Palazoac slime," as Callaway calls it, had spilled over into a vast flood plain, deflected there by the coriolis effect, the influence of the earth's rotation on objects moving over its surface, which causes motion in the northern hemisphere to be thrown to the right. In the river are shad, chain pickerel, skipjack herring, spotted suckers, golden shiners, channel catfish, yellow bullheads, Atlantic needlefish, striped mullet, brook silversides, white bass, redbreast and redear sunfish, black crappie, largemouth bass, hog chokers, and gulf flounder. Four-hundred-pound sturgeon come from halfway around the world to spawn in the Apalachicola. It drains 19,600 square miles, twice the area of any other river in Florida, and is the clean, wild river I was unable to find on my search throughout the peninsula. Industry and destruction were catching up with it, though. A hundred miles from the Gulf, five from the headwaters of the Apalachicola, Jackson County was dredging a port and a manufacturing zone to create new jobs to awaken a sleeping economy and to keep home the children who were fleeing the area as soon as they got out of school. By this time, I wouldn't be surprised if heavy barges laden with paper, plastics, chemicals, and other goods are plying the length of the Apalachicola.

Roy Clay helped me out with the trees of the deep riverine forest. "Let me tell you something, Mr. White Man. You see that tree down there yonder in that slough? That's a elum." He had names for some I'd never heard before. I'd heard white pine called old field pine, but never rosemary pine. Loblolly pine to him was black pine, and turkey oak was jack oak, plain and simple. I wandered down into one of the ravines which Callaway had referred to, poetically, as "glens and dells," but which Roy Clay insisted were "vinyons." It was February. The forest plants were at a stage of awakening that would not reach New England for another six weeks. Below the plantation house the red buckeye was putting on leaves down by some overgrown Confederate gun pits. Wake-robin trilliums were out, and certain spots on the forest floor had favored the purple and white and yellow blooms of toothwort, violet, bloodroot, and troutlily. The broad, glossy leaves of four kinds of magnolia shone above them, and dogwood, wild hydrangea, Carolina silverbell, Ogeechee tupelo, persimmon, holly, and the rare Florida yew also stood in the shade of the big trees, some of which were in water. Many of the bald cypresses, tulips, sweet gums, tupelo gums, wild pecans, walnuts, hickories, swamp maples, and swamp chestnut oaks were colossal and, I suspect, virgin.

On one of the limestone slopes I found a tough little gymnosperm several feet high, bristling with sharp, flat needles that would have drawn blood if I had stuck myself. Instead I crushed a few of the

needles, and they smelled like tomatoes on the vine. The branchlets form perfect crosses with the branches, and for this reason Callaway considers this species holy. It was a gopherwood, also known as Florida torreya, stinking cedar, stinking savern, and savernwood, the last of which is what Roy Clay calls it. The tree was discovered in 1821 by young Dr. John Torrey of New York. Its wood is very light and very strong. After five hundred years its trunk gets to have a girth of twenty inches, big enough to use for building an ark. Local people use it for fence posts, though. It has no commercial value. About ten years ago all the gopherwood trees in Bristol were struck by a mysterious blight and died. Now there remain only little suckers from the roots, like the one there before me. E. E. Callaway's theory is that the trees weren't needed any more, so God simply took them away. "That tree was for one purpose, to save man from the flood. But God said he would never destroy man by flood again, and that's why he put a rainbow in the sky. Since he's not going to destroy us again he hasn't any further need for the gopherwood. God wants to put that land to some other use."

Having dallied in the forest a good bit of the day I pressed on, hoping to reach Panama City by nightfall. After driving quite a while I sighted a great blue heron gliding over the treetops, and then a sign saying WAVECREST HOTEL, 5 MI. I must be reaching the sea. Yep. Soon the forest gave way to a gray area of small businesses and slums. Signs for Panama City began to crop up. I parted company at a V with a black man who had just gotten out of the Veterans Hospital in Ocala. He put out his thumb for a ride downtown, where he was fixing to land a job as a short-order cook, and I made for the water.

If I ever have to lay low for a while, I'll probably do it in Panama City. The place is big enough that you could live here inconspicuously, but sufficiently in the sticks that the past would have a time catching up with you. The Panama City Chamber of Commerce calls it "Florida's Best-Kept Secret," because vacations and retirement are cheaper here than anywhere else in the state. Furnished apartments, comfy bungalows, and motel accommodations rent for as little as sixty dollars a month. The average family income is one of the lowest in the country, in spite of various schemes for improving the area, which include starting up a catfish farm and building a reef out of old car bodies to boost commercial fishing. Industry has been invited too, but until it responds, the mainstays of Bay County continue to be the Tyndall Air Force Base and the International Paper Company, which employ seven and ten thousand, respectively.

Panama City's young, aggressive tourist industry is largely concentrated on a "Miracle Strip" along St. Andrew Bay. Maybe because I had only just emerged from the vinyons of Torreya State Park, the strip struck me as one of the bleakest outcrops of human enterprise upon which I have ever laid eyes. It gets a lot of business from landlocked southern states like Kentucky and Tennessee and the inland parts of Georgia and Alabama, but its presence is a mixed blessing to the local populace. They see only that their beaches are crowded and their roads torn up by out-of-state traffic, and that they have to pay for the repairs out of their own taxes, while the profits go to the nomadic tribe of motelkeepers and concessionaires that appear whenever there is a new tourist mecca to be established. Early in the summer of 1972, when Hurricane Agnes passed through, the Miracle Strip was miraculously spared, and the merchants got together and sued the U.S. Weather Bureau for issuing reports that frightened their business away. Further east along Route 98, hundreds of houses on the Gulf were torn to pieces.

Adjoining the Miracle Strip, out on a spit, is St. Andrew State Park. I got there in time for a sunset swim with some Portuguese men-of-war in the Grand Lagoon of the bay. Across it, about five miles away, the illuminated stacks of the International Paper mill spewed up black plumes of smoke that joined a dull gray blanket of discoloration already filling most of the sky. I caught a whiff of methyl mercaptan and hydrogen sulfide, the rotten-egg smell that is the unfortunate residue of the kraft papermaking process. On streets near the mill, fumes have peeled the paint on a number of houses and blackened the trees. But the people of Panama City feel they can't afford to be too fussy about their environment, and they accept the fumes as part of life, calling them "the smell of money." There's still a warm feeling toward the mill, which pulled Bay County out of the depression in 1929. The oldest paper plant in Florida, it has stood there forty-three years, rolling out a hundred and fifty tons of pulp and linerboard a day; "a tribute to modern American manufacturing genius," if the International Paper Company does say so itself.

Next morning I dropped by the mill for a meeting with Jim Mann, who had recently been transferred from the company's installation in Birmingham, Alabama, to become their p.r. man in Panama City. Among his other activities he puts out the Panama City *Kraft Messenger*, a tabloid for the millhands. The latest issue carried a picture of a man in bib overalls named Homer Bozemann, who had retired after forty-seven years in the woodlands. In the *Messenger* "Yuk-yuks" section I came across a roast-hippie joke:

A cannibal opened a restaurant. In the window he put a sign that read men—$1.55; women—$2.20; hippies—$25.00. A customer went in and asked the owner why it cost so much to order a 'hippie.' The cannibal replied, "Did you ever try to clean one of them rascals?"

We sat in Jim's office drinking coffee from Styrofoam cups while he explained a few things. "In the first place, the paper industry has never been a great money maker. When business is good, you make a little. When it ain't, you don't make a thing. About forty-five percent of the mills in America are economically marginal by current standards of efficiency. The old mills are usually the shakiest, as well as being the worst polluters, and in a few years we expect sixteen thousand people to be laid off from mills that it makes more sense to shut down than to bring up to the new antipollution standards. This here mill, though, is in no danger of folding, even though it's one of the old ones. The company has too big an investment in it. In fact we're sinking twenty million more into it—seventeen million for two new recovery boilers, which will recover ninety-nine percent of the spent chemicals and ashes and keep them from being discharged from the stacks as particulate matter. Another three million is earmarked for water-pollution abatement. Now, our waste water has three problems: it is hot, it contains fibers, and it lacks almost any oxygen, so that the fish in the stream into which it is discharged eventually suffocate.

"We eliminated the first two problems in fifty-five by building a three-hundred-foot-diameter cement settling basin in which the water is left for eleven hours before being released into the East Bay. This process, which is called primary treatment, allows the fibers, resin, and starch to sludge out and be transported back to be burned with the bark instead of settling out in the bay and killing off the fish and plants. It also gives the water a chance to cool off, so by the time it enters the bay it's only a few degrees warmer than the ocean. But we're still working on the lack-of-oxygen problem. Primary treatment reduces about ten to thirty percent of the water's biological oxygen demand, or BOD, but that's still not enough for the fish to live on. So now we're installing a three-million-dollar secondary-treatment system. The waste water will be pumped from the settling basin through a pipeline to the Tyndall Air Force Base across the bay, where we've leased a hundred acres for an aeration lagoon that will churn the oxygen back into the water with great big eggbeaters."

At that point the noon whistle blew, and we went to grab a bite at the mill lunchroom. Laying our hard hats on the floor by our chairs, we dug into some short ribs and collard greens. There were a few blacks at one table, two musclebound longhairs at another, and the rest of the room was occupied by maybe twenty middle-aged southern rednecks. Most of the men were talking about five hundred gallons of oil that had been spilled into the bay that morning from a tanker. They'd gotten out there with ropes and floats and corralled the spill, thrown out a mess of pulp to soak it up, hauled it ashore, and scooped it up with a 'dozer. The captain of the tanker had been blamed for the incident, arrested, and freed on five hundred dollars bail. He had jumped bail and shipped out an hour ago.

Jim now took me into the mill itself, a huge room filled with vats and deafening machinery. Technically, he explained, the Panama City mill is known as a "two-machine board mill." One of the machines makes unbleached linerboard, which is used for the outside liners of cardboard boxes, and the other turns out bleached machine-dried hardwood pulp whose trade name is International A–02 Supercell. These two machines were running side by side, spinning endless ribbons of brown linerboard and white Supercell through eighty drying cylinders at the rate of fifteen hundred feet per minute, twenty-four hours a day, all year round, except for thirteen days when the mill is closed for holidays. The ribbons are taken off in gigantic reels weighing several tons apiece and are cut into appropriate sizes for shipping. Most of the linerboard goes by rail to Auburndale, the cardboard capital of Florida, where it is incorporated into corrugated boxes. The Supercell is shipped to seventy-one ports in thirty-two countries and winds up as all kinds of things: typewriter paper, sanitary napkins, blotter paper in the Philippines and other countries where blotters have yet to be displaced by the ballpoint pen.

One of the troubles with these machines is their noise. The mill-hands are advised to wear earplugs, but even those who do become victims of premature deafness and fainting spells which are symptoms of a shattered nervous system. Yet, in the middle of this ruckus, pigeons were strutting on the loading dock, and others had nestled under the rafters. If the noise had bothered them enough, I suppose they could have flown away.

Jim conducted me into the wood yard on a springy, soggy carpet of bark shavings. The yard was the size of several football fields, piled high with pulpwood of various kinds and lengths. Most of it, he explained, comes by truck and rail from farmers in southern Alabama and Georgia, who make it through the winter by harvesting their woodlots. About thirty percent comes from the company's four-hundred-thousand-acre holdings in the Panhandle. It is deliv-

A Typical Florida Beach

F7

ered in uncut poles, or longwood, if it is harvested mechanically, and in five-foot lengths if the work is done by hand. Thirty to forty mill days of wood are always kept in reserve in case rain slows delivery.

The timber was sorted into hard- and softwood. Mixed stacks of yellow pine—slash, loblolly, sand, longleaf, and shortleaf—the height of several men, stood next to heaps of oak and gum and other hardwoods of which I could only recognize the distinctive barks of sycamore and beech. The pine fibers are three millimeters long on the average, longer and tougher than those of the hardwoods, and are used for linerboard. The hardwood fibers are one millimeter long, smoother, and have better printing characteristics than those of the pines. They are converted into Supercell.

There has always been a surplus of hardwood timber suitable for pulp in the South, Jim told me. Many of the sixty commercial species grow on a variety of sites ranging from swamps to steep slopes. It was not until after the Second World War that bulldozers, caterpillars, and other heavy equipment for dragging them out were developed, and mills began to use hardwood extensively. Now some mills run sixty percent hardwood.

These hardwood harvests are mostly one-shot deals. It is more profitable for a farmer to replant his woodlot with faster-growing pine or soybeans, and the conversion of forests into food crops is only going to increase as we keep producing more hungry mouths to feed. In the process, the old deciduous stands in the Panhandle are shrinking, and their loss is felt by all who have come under their spell. Only patches of the pre-Columbian woods, like the trees I stood beneath in Torreya State Park, remain. Most of it has been replaced with plantations of hybrid slash-loblolly pine. The seedlings in this pine monoculture won't reach merchantable size till after

1990, and meanwhile the paper industry is expected to run through the existing natural stands of merchantable hardwood timber by 1880.

We watched a man who had been napping in the cab of a crane awake, swivel his scoop over to a pile of the dwindling hardwoods, and drop it on them unceremoniously. The big jaws opened and clamped down on the trees. The man yawned, pulled some levers, and lifted the trees over to a conveyor belt, which carried them first to the debarking drums and then to the chippers. They were shredded to bits in seconds.

Billbored

Below Atlanta the unsuspecting snowbird progressing south on I–75 plunges into a forest of billboards which gets him so worked up about Florida, that, by the time he crosses the border, his vacation is liable to be an anticlimax. And by the time he shoots over Payne's Prairie, eight miles below Gainesville, the billboards have gotten so thick that he may fail to notice one of the great natural wonders of central Florida. Named for King Payne, a Seminole chief who was killed by U.S. troops in 1812, Payne's Prairie is a twelve-thousand-acre sea of tall grasses and sedges, in a depression surrounded by bluffs. At various times water has invaded the prairie, bubbling up from a great sinkhole at its center, transforming it into a lake. The last time this happened was in the twenties. But one day the lake just plain disappeared into the sink, and it hasn't been seen since. Many older people remember walking out with baskets and collecting the stranded fish.

When the Philadelphia botanist William Bartram crossed the prairie in 1774, there was not a lake but a wet savanna grazed by the wild cattle of the Seminoles. Bartram and his party spent a few days crossing it, during which he described seeing "at the same time . . . innumerable droves of cattle; the lordly bull, lowing cow and sleek capricious heifer. The hills and groves re-echo their cheerful, social voices. Herds of sprightly deer, squadrons of the beautiful, fleet Siminole [sic] horse, flocks of turkeys, civilized communities of the sonorous, watchful savanna crane, mix together, appearing happy and contented in the enjoyment of peace, till disturbed and affrighted by the warrior man." Bartram must have been greatly impressed with "the magnificent plains of Alachua," as he called the prairie. He wrote how "on the first view of such an amazing display of the wisdom and power of the supreme author of nature, the mind for a moment seems suspended, and impressed with awe."

Today the prairie is grazed by cattle, which help keep down the willows and buttonbushes. After every rain, there sprout in the cow paddies certain hallucinogenic mushrooms which also grow in Mexico, where they have been used by Indians in religious ceremonies since before 1500. When eight or nine of them are eaten, their active ingredient, psilocybin, produces rushes of brilliant color that last about eight hours, after which most people come down, though some haven't come down yet. Hundreds of long-haired pilgrims make it to Gainesville to get high on these coprophilic fungi. And there is a certain U-Totem shopping mart in town in front of which people who have tripped on the fabulous "shrooms" sit and discuss their religious experiences.

Early in 1972 Payne's Prairie was acquired by the State Department of Natural Resources, which promptly closed it off to the public. The Fish and Game Commission bugged it with microphones to study the movements of the wildlife before determining what uses the park should be put to. It wants to remove the cows because they are not part of the native wildlife, but it will then have to substitute some other way of keeping the prairie from growing up. One idea is to burn it periodically. In 1971, eleven thousand five hundred acres in seventeen state parks underwent controlled or "ecological" burning, which is used to maintain the diversity of plant communities in places where men have interfered with the natural fire cycles. Another thought is to reintroduce the bison, which once roamed the plains of Central Florida.

One evening I put the top down and drove out to the prairie with two brothers from Gainesville, one's girlfriend, and their dog. Since no one was allowed on the savanna itself, we parked and walked out along Highway 441. This road cuts right through the prairie half a mile or so from Interstate 75, and at night the animals trying to cross it are slaughtered in great numbers. We found dozens of road kills: small marsh rabbits, which were everywhere this year, water snakes, a round-tailed muskrat, a possum, and a three-lined stink-jim turtle, not more than four inches long. Halfway across the prairie we came across a camper pulled onto the shoulder and two women screaming excitedly while a boy was running after something in the grass, and then jumping back when he got to it, as if he couldn't make up his mind what to do. It was a large snake, about four feet long, and the boy had a tire iron in his hand. The women were trying to get him to bludgeon the critter, but he was scared stiff of it. Steve, one of my passengers, walked over, picked up the snake by the middle and held it in the air, letting it slither up on itself. Then it glided along his arm, and you could see its belly was as pink as salmon flesh. "He won't hurt you. There's no way in the world you can get this snake to bite you."

"Wha'? That ain't a moccasin?" the boy asked.

"Heck no. This is a horned snake. It eats moccasins. One of the friendliest snakes there is," Steve said, holding up its tail and showing the boy its horny integument. "He'd make a great pet, except you probably couldn't get him to eat anything."

Gradually the boy got over some of his fear and put out his hand to touch the snake's tail. Three dudes on motorcycles stopped to watch. The boy swallowed hard and let Steve drape the snake around his shoulders like a shawl. He looked at the two women nervously, and the muscles of his right arm shuddered involuntarily as the critter slithered down it. He managed a grin. "Hey, man," he said shakily, "I didn't know. I thought it was a moccasin. Thanks."

The prairie was teeming with life, most of which couldn't be seen. But we could hear gallinules chuckling in the grass, and occasionally a great blue heron, or a little blue, or an anhinga, or an egret would rise up from a pool where it had been wading among lotuses. On the far edge we could see a tree whitened with ibises, which had already roosted there for the night. Tomorrow at dawn, at some silent telepathic command, or more likely when the sun reached a critical angle, they would fly up in one body and begin their day.

There were two things I especially wanted to see on the prairie. I would have liked to find some of the psilocybin mushrooms. But we were in a dry spell, and rain is needed for the fruition of basidiomycetes. I was also hoping to catch a glimpse of Bartram's "sonorous savanna crane." This is a more appropriate name for the birds than their modern one, sandhill crane, because they actually spend

EAT AT SARRES' - DRIVE INN AND RESTAURANT - 1926 SILVER SPRINGS BLVD., OCALA, FLORIDA

FOR STEAKS, CHICKEN, FROG LEGS AND SEA FOODS

most of their time on wet flats. When he visited the prairie Bartram saw thousands of them "in well disciplined squadrons, now rising from the earth, mount aloft in spiral circles, far above the dense atmosphere of the humid plain; they again view the glorious sun, and the light of day still gleaming on their polished feathers, they sing their evening hymn, then in a strait line majestically descend, and alight on the towering Palms or lofty Pines, their secure and peaceful resting places."

The cranes are almost five feet tall when they stand up, which makes them an easy mark, and their food is mostly vegetable, which makes them tasty. So naturally there aren't many around any more. But a few dozen are making a last stand on the prairie. I wanted to hear their "evening hymn," which from all reports is an unforgettable yodel you can pick up a mile away. We drove around the prairie to several strategic locations, but heard nothing that made an impression on us. Just as we had given up we passed two big smoky-gray birds browsing in a pool with their heads down. They looked up to check us out, showing their red foreheads and crowns. We passed around the binoculars, and when they came to me I took a good look. Then I zoomed in on the background. Half a mile behind them, a procession of billboards, dozens deep and in serried ranks, marched on a raised embankment across the prairie.

"Holy crow!" I gasped. "What's that?"

"That," Steve informed me, "is I-75."

From Gainesville to the Route 27 exit in Silver Springs, a distance of twenty-odd miles, the southbound passenger on I-75 is confronted with a billboard every few seconds—two hundred sixty-seven all told when I passed that way. It was a dazzling assortment: sixty-two eating establishments, sixty-two gas stations, thirty-four campgrounds, twenty-seven motels, one cafeteria chain, one deer ranch, one preparatory school, two beaches, one suntan lotion, one magic kingdom (Disney World), one divinity (GET RIGHT WITH GOD), one land sale, one modern art center, four award-winning mobile-home communities, one thoroughbred breeders' association, two handbag factories, three western towns, five counties, six antique stores, one Sears Roebuck, one tropical wonderland, two aquatariums, one bank, one circus, one reptile institute, one farm bureau, one jai alai stadium, one university football schedule, one trailer park, one old ship, one aqua pier, thirteen springs, two home sites, two welcome centers, two mobile-home shows, eight mill outlets, seven gardens, some sunken and some not, and four blanks with nothing on them whatever.

The amazing thing is that every single one of these signs is illegal. Billboards were the prime target of Lady Bird Johnson's beautification program when she was first lady of the land, and in 1965 she got Congress to pass a federal law prohibiting any signs within 660 feet of the outside edge of the right of way on any interstate or other highway receiving primary federal aid. This so-called Lady Bird Act was ratified by the Florida State Legislature in December, 1971. Now there are more billboards in Florida than in any other state of the union except California. At the rate of anywhere from a hundred to five thousand dollars apiece it is going to cost about forty million to compensate the outdoor advertising agencies for all the condemned billboards. Seventy-five percent of the amount will be paid by the federal government, but the other twenty-five has to be raised by upping the state tax on gasoline. Billboards that are judged unsightly or hazardous, that have not been kept up or that might blow down in the wind, will not be compensated, however.

As soon as the word was out that their billboards were about to be bought, the ad agencies erected two thousand more on I–75 between Gainesville and Disney World. They also put up mammoth billboards beyond the six-hundred-sixty-foot limit and actually poisoned with herbicide any trees in the state right of way that obstructed their view. But the Department of Transportation decided that no billboard erected after the Lady Bird Act was ratified would be compensated, and filed suits against ad agencies in four counties for destroying public trees. The people who drafted the Lady Bird Act now regret the six-hundred-sixty-foot clause. The law as it went on the books favors the people who can afford elephantine signs, discriminates against the little businessman, and results in even further defacing of the environment.

While passengers on the interstates may soon be able to open their eyes again to the unreal beauty of places like Payne's Prairie, many other Florida roads will continue to be plastered with billboards. One morning I drove on Route 1 from Key Largo to Key West, picking up a bum who was carrying a blanket roll, an overcoat, a sterno stove, a hand line, and a small skillet. He'd started out from New London, Connecticut, a few months earlier, had worked his way to Guadalajara, Mexico, and was now on his way to Key West, which is a great mecca for bums. Off in the water, brilliant fish grazed in the tropical sea gardens, rocking back and forth in the swells. A school of several thousand fry rose and peppered the azure water. Up in the trees of Plantation Key a startled little girl with ribbons in her hair was having her bikini pulled down over her bottom by a cocker spaniel, and a text read, TAN DON'T BURN. Down the road a piece a gigantic topless grownup was lying on her belly in the sand urging you to MAKE YOUR FLORIDA TAN BROWN AND BEAUTIFUL.

Somewhat further on an apparently incautious sunbather was wincing as she peeled her strap from her raw, scalded shoulder, while the caption said, SOLARCAINE FOR SUNBURN PAIN. Lower Matecumbe Key had another brand: COMPASSION STOPS SUNBURN PAIN IN SECONDS; a big hand was spraying the stuff on an Indian-red female back.

During the long, lonely hours of driving below Tallahassee, I would occasionally come across series of signs spaced fifty feet apart, written in alternate red and black capitals:

NEW CROP PECANS 3 lb./$1.00

PECAN MEATS HOT ROASTED PEANUTS

TUPELO HONEY ORANGE BLOSSOM HONEY

PECAN ROLLS 4/$1.00

PECAN GLAZE SUGAR SPICE PECANS

FINEST PAPER SHELL PECANS

HOT ROASTED PEANUTS

SHELLED PECANS 99¢ PER BAG

NEW CROP PECANS 3lb./$1.00

When I got to the Pecan House, it turned out to be made entirely of signs:

PECANS 3lb./$1.00

HOME GROWN PECANS

HOT PEANUTS

Peaches in Miami Beach, Florida 71

And, after all that, it seemed they were out of pecans.

Sometimes as I tooled along I would come across a sign planted right in a swamp, then one in a flatwoods, and a few more on a prairie where Brahman cows wandered through the morning mist. One sequence went

FOLKS
I'M AGIN
ROAD SIGNS
BUT HOW

ELSE
Y'ALL GONNA
KNOW WHERE
T' GO

FER
TH BEST
PIT BAR-B-Q
N'TH'SOUTH

OLD
SOUTH
BAR-B-Q
RANCH

No matter where I was, a billboard was only a moment away.

GET US OUT OF THE UNITED NATIONS
SEND $2.00 FOR SPECIAL U.N. PACKET

One big one outside of Tampa on Route 688 expressed concern for the environment:

$$E = MC^2$$
$$ECOLOGY = MAN + CONCERN^2$$

It seems like the future of Florida is written on these signs—signs for big developments that offer free shells or orange juice, signs that say

BOB HINES PRESTIGE HOMES AND PROPERTIES

or

FUTURE SIGHT OF BANO

or

RAMADA INN COMING SOON

or

BUILDING AN ALL-NEW WINN-DIXIE

or, on the Kissimmee Prairie, west of St. Cloud and still miles from anywhere:

12,000 ACRES FOR SALE OR LEASE
CONTACT BARRY SHUMAN
CHICAGO, ILLIN.

How I Sold My Car for a Coke

Late one afternoon I checked into Weir's Motor Court at Coral Gables and was given the key to cabin number 10. I stood in the shower for a while, then fell out on the bed. Two women with their hair in curlers walked by the window, one with a baby in her arms. The sky was overcast with cumulonimbus clouds, and the room had a peculiar aroma. There was a ghost image on the television. Down the street somebody was tuning an electric guitar. The whole block was for rent, as far as I could see—prefabricated apartments and rundown motor courts with screen porches where the tenants could sit in the evening.

As I lay there I gradually realized it was time for me to split. It was time to clear out of this hot-dog circus world, so exotic in some ways and so contemptibly familiar in others. Sixty-two days on the road was plenty, and I was beginning to wake up in the morning with cold shudders. I missed my dog. I missed winter, stone walls, and a sense of the past. I know a woods near my hometown where you can sit at dusk and listen to the liquid fluting of wood thrushes, watch fireflies light up, and smell wild azaleas at the same time. Florida had been just fine, but to my way of thinking, this old woods just beat anything *I'd* seen.*

So I packed up my tropical kit and headed north. South of Palatka I picked up a long-haired journeyman welder who was hitching up from Tampa to visit his folks for the weekend. We passed a crazy old man standing in the middle of the road waving wildly, with a gunnysack for a hat and snow-white hair grazing his shoulders. I've seen others like him, standing out there, directing imaginary traffic with the far-off gleam of inexpressible wisdom; old duffers who must have remembered the roads when there wasn't a car on them. There's one such in my hometown who took it upon himself one day to neaten up the burying ground by pulling the honeysuckle from the old stone tablets there. Another time, he lined the village green with white-painted boulders, and the only thanks he got for that were complaints lodged by several of the townspeople about their unsightliness.

---

*Eight months later, much to my surprise, I found myself back in Florida again, checking out a few facts. I dropped in on Coral Gables but couldn't find Weir's Motor Court. I went back to Immokalee too and found the flophouse where I'd spent New Year's Eve burned to the ground. In Orlando the Baba Sirchand ashram was deserted, except for a Muscovy duck waddling around the premises. All the windows had been smashed and torn clothes were scattered in the driveway. I met a boy cutting across the lot on his way home from school. He told me the place had been sold to a builder of condominiums. One evening I was cruising Route 441, looking for a cement-tepee motel village I'd passed on my last trip. It, too, had been condemned and razed. The man pumping gas across the street hadn't even noticed that the teepees weren't there any more.

A "JOY RIDE" IN FLORIDA

My rider admired the way I drive at a steady fifty m.p.h., slow enough so you can put your left foot up on the dash and take in the passing countryside. I told him I always travel the old U.S. highway system unless I'm particularly pressed for time, because you can't see anything from the interstates and if you take your eyes off the road for a second you're liable to be killed. "Yup," he said, putting his feet up on the dash too, "I reckon this is the way to travel."

As I drove I remembered a diary that had fallen into my brother's possession. Kept by a woman from Wingdale, New York, during a trip to Florida she and her husband had made during the depression, it told how they set out in a Buick convertible with only two dollars between them, how they would steal knives and forks from one diner and sell them to the next in exchange for a meal, how they siphoned gas from parked cars and slept in abandoned tarpaper shacks, how she gave birth to a girl in the back seat, how they picked fruit and vegetables for a winter and returned to Wingdale the following spring. Somehow, I don't know why, I felt a real kinship with them.

I don't recall whether the diary mentioned anything about a radio or not. My convertible had a radio, but it was on the blink, I imagine with a wornout tube. So I left it on all the time, and about once a week I'd go over a bump and it would come on with some bulletin from the outside world, about one or another local P.T.A. meeting or a rattlesnake roundup, or it would play one of the top ten, or announce that it was seventy-seven muggy degrees in downtown wherever it happened to be.

The only good things that ever come out of Detroit, as far as I'm concerned, are convertibles, and most of Detroit isn't even making them any more. They're victims of air pollution and street punks and people who'd rather have air-conditioning running up their legs than feel the wind in their faces. Detroit has been responsible for all sorts of things you never would have imagined, like dust bowls, for instance. When cars displaced horses as the way to get around, the vast oat and barley fields in the Midwest that were sown to feed the quadrupeds were abandoned. The oat and barley root systems that held the fields in place shriveled up, the wind blew off the topsoil, and that is how the great dust storms of the thirties came into being, I'm told. Now there's hardly a place in the country that's exempt from the sound of a passing car.

"You know it seems to me, maybe, what we've gained by all these short cuts we have doesn't amount to nothing compared to what we've lost," my passenger from Tampa said thoughtfully. Suddenly the purple bus ahead of us, carrying the Harvesters for Christ on a soul-saving foray, slowed down, and a highway patrolman flagged us around a head-on collision that had just happened. The ambulance was there already and three police cruisers were throwing out spasmodic blue flashes into the flatwoods. A dozen carloads of rubberneckers were watching two men in white pick a limp figure out of the wreck. My friend shook his head and said, "Cars are nothing but oversized bullets. They kill you just as sure. They got two of my buddies and put another one in a wheelchair for life."

Now let me give you a quick rundown on my cream-colored '64 Oldsmobile Dynamic 88. I bought her in October '71 for two hundred dollars and drove her around for the first two months unregistered, uninsured, uninspected, unkempt, and, after my New Hampshire schoolbus driver's license ran out, unlicensed. I heard the cops in the South don't mess around, so I cleaned up the act and got her legalized, and she took me twice to Florida and once to Carville,

Louisiana. One day I was sitting at my mom's kitchen window with Walt Koken, the finest old-time country fiddler in Upper New York State, if not the world, trying to figure out a name for the Olds. We threw out a couple to see what they sounded like: Sally, Carolina, Big Jane, The Gyrene. But none of them seemed to do justice to her long, sleek magnificence. Finally old Walt hiked up his jeans and said, "Why don't you call her Georgia?" And, by Jesus, that was that.

Now, Georgia was a car in a million. I only saw two other '64 Oldsmobile Dynamic 88s in the fifteen thousand miles I had her, and one of them was a hard top. I figured if she got me back from Florida this time I'd have the old crate gold-plated and mounted on a pedestal. And just to make sure she'd make it okay I pulled into a station one day in South Carolina and had the oil changed, and that turned out to be her undoing. The mechanic was a nice guy, but he didn't tighten the oil plug, and it must have fallen out on the road, because thirty miles later, at 11:43 A.M., on July 30, 1972, in the northbound lane of I–95, old Georgia, without a drop of oil in her crank case, seized and ground to a halt just short of a bridge. My Dynamic 88 became a static 88, as it were, and it was all over for Georgia. Two boys from Bob's Garage came in a wrecker and towed her in solemn silence to Manning, South Carolina, where I signed her over to Bob himself in exchange for one Coke, which I drank on the spot. I told the boys they could divvy up my collapsible sun-deck chair, my seersucker suit, my mosquito net, my badminton racket, and the rest of my tropical kit, and they gave me a lift to the Gulf station, where I waited for the Trailways bus with a black flyboy whose leave had terminated. And I reckon that's about the size of it.

ABOUT THE AUTHOR

Alex Shoumatoff, a staff writer for *The New Yorker*, is the author of seven previous books, including *In Southern Light*, *The Rivers Amazon*, *Russian Blood*, and *African Madness* (both available from Vintage). He has an abiding interest in the Third World tropics and the relationship between man and nature. He is the father of two boys and now resides in Mexico City.

Also by

Alex Shoumatoff

African Madness

Brilliantly written, filled with horror, sadness, and a sense of wonder,
these four essays take us to Rwanda, to reconsider the life and savage
death of the primatologist Dian Fossey...to Madagascar, an endangered
Eden of impossible life forms...to the Central African Republic, to the
trial of "the emperor who ate his people"...and across tropical Africa in
search of the origins of AIDS.

Russian Blood
A Family Chronicle

Alex Shoumatoff traces his family's origins back to Russia in the fifteenth
century. He imaginatively re-creates his ancestors' lives, enthusiasms, and
disappointments; their buffetings by war and revolution; their survival in
America before World War II and after. *Russian Blood* is a memoir that
says volumes about the nature of all families, everywhere.